Christmas is coming
    The goose is getting fat,
Please put a penny
    In the old man's hat.
If you haven't got a penny
    A ha'penny will do,
If you haven't got a ha'penny,
    God bless you.

THE BOOK OF
CHRISTMAS

Edited by Neil Philip
Illustrated by Sally Holmes

STEWART, TABORI & CHANG
NEW YORK

Published in 1991 by Stewart, Tabori & Chang, Inc.
575 Broadway
New York, NY 10012

An Albion Book
Designer: Emma Bradford
Project co-ordinator: Elizabeth Wilkes

Library of Congress Cataloging-in-Publication Data
The Book of Christmas / edited by Neil Philip : illustrated by Sally
Holmes.
p.   cm.
ISBN 1-55670-188-8
1. Christmas—Literary collections.   I. Philip, Neil.
II. Holmes, Sally.
PN6071.C6B618   1991
808.8′033—dc20   91-12118
CIP

Distributed in the U.S. by Workman Publishing
708 Broadway, New York, NY 10003
Distributed in Canada by Canadian Manda Group
P.O. Box 920, Station U, Toronto, Ontario M8Z 5P9

Typesetting and color origination by York House, London
Printed and bound in Hong Kong by South China Printing Co.

10 9 8 7 6 5 4 3 2 1

First edition

CONTENTS

For my mother and for my father
S.H.
For Elizabeth
N.P.

WINTER'S SONG

TRADITIONAL

Translated from the Bohemian

Drop down, drop down, white snowflakes!
We shall hide ourselves in fur coats
And when the blizzard comes
We shall put on fur caps,
We shall harness our golden sleighs,
We shall drive down from our hillside
And if we fall into a snowdrift
We hope that the wind will not cover us,
So that we can drive back quickly
For the fairy tales which grandfather will tell us.

THE SNOWMAN

HANS CHRISTIAN ANDERSEN

Translated by Brian Alderson

"I'm all of a crackle inside with this scrumptious cold!" said the snowman. "The wind really blows a bit of life into you! And how that glowing thing glowers!" (He meant the sun, which was just about to set.) "He'll not make me blink; I can still keep hold of my bits and pieces."

He was talking about two big, triangular bits of tile, which were his eyes; his mouth was part of an old rake, so that he'd got teeth. He'd been born to the sound of boys cheering and greeted with the jingle of sleigh-bells and the cracking of whips.

The sun set. The full moon came up, big and round, shining white and beautiful in the darkening air. "Here he comes again from the other side," said the snowman. (He thought it was the sun come up again.) "I saw him off with all his glowering! Now he can hang up there and shine away so that I can see myself. If only I knew how people moved and got about! I'd very much like to get about myself! If I could, I'd go down there and slide on the ice like I saw the boys doing; but I don't know how to run."

"Grroff! Grroff!" barked the old watchdog. He was a bit hoarse, which had happened since the days when he'd been a house-dog and lain by the fire. "The sun'll teach you how to run! I saw that with the chap who was here before you – and with the chap before him. Grroff! Grroff! Everybody grroff!"

"Now then, friend, I don't know what you're talking about!" said the snowman. "Him up there teach me to run?" (He meant the moon.) "Oh, yes! He was running himself right enough last time I looked at him; now he's sneaking back from the other side."

"You're stupid," said the watchdog, "but then you've only just been slapped together! What you're looking at now is called the moon; the sun was the one before. He'll come again tomorrow morning and he'll teach you to run down there into the ditch by the wall. We're in for a change of weather – I can tell because I get pains in my left back leg. We're in for a shift of weather."

"I don't know what he's talking about at all," said the snowman, "but

I've got an idea that it's not something nice. That thing that glowered and then disappeared, that he called the sun, he's certainly no friend of mine – I can feel it in my bones."

"Grroff! Grroff!" barked the watchdog, turned himself round three times, and lay down in the kennel to go to sleep.

And a change in the weather really did come. Towards morning there was a thick, clammy mist over everything; then later the wind got up – icy cold – the frost gripped everything. But what a

sight it was when the sun came up! All the trees and bushes were covered with hoar-frost, like a whole forest of white coral, where all the twigs bloomed with glittering white flames. The delicate tracery of branches, that you can't see in summer because of all the leaves, now showed up clearly. It was like lace, and so gleaming white, with white lights glimmering from every twig. The birch tree lifted its branches in the wind, live, like the trees in summer; it was wonderfully beautiful! And when the sun shone down everything sparkled as if it was powdered with a dust of diamonds, with big diamonds glinting in the drifts of snow. You'd think that

countless little lights were burning, whiter than the white snow.

"That is wonderfully beautiful," said a young girl, coming out into the garden with a young man and standing next to the snowman, looking at the glittering trees. "You wouldn't see it so beautiful, even in summer!" she said, and her eyes sparkled.

"And you won't have a fellow like this here then," said the young man, and he pointed to the snowman. "He's splendid."

The young girl laughed, nodded at the snowman and danced off with her friend over the snow, which crunched under her as though she was walking on starch.

"Who were those two?" the snow-man asked the watchdog. "You've been on this farm longer than I have, do you know 'em?"

"Of course I do!" said the watch-dog. "She's patted me and he's given me bones; I don't bite them."

"But what are they up to here?"

asked the snowman.

"Courrrr – , courrrr – , courting!"said the watchdog. "They'll be moving into the same kennel and gnawing bones together. Grroff! Grroff!"

"And are those two as important as you and me?" asked the snowman.

"They belong to the guvnor," said the watchdog. "Really, people born yesterday are an ignorant lot, and you're one of 'em! As for me – I've got age and wisdom; I know everything that's going on at this farm! And what's more, I know a time when I wasn't chained up out here in the cold. Grroff! Grroff!"

"The cold's very nice," said the snowman. "But come on, tell me all about it – only don't keep rattling your chain, it gives me the willies inside."

"Grroff! Grroff!" barked the watchdog. "I was young once; 'Oh, isn't he a sweet little thing', they used to say, and I lay in a velvet chair up there in the farmhouse, lay in the guvnor's lap. They used to kiss my nose and wipe my paws with an embroidered handkerchief and it was all 'prettykins' and 'dear little woofums'. But then I got too big for them, so they gave me to the housekeeper and I had to live in the basement! You can see where it was from where you're standing; you can see down into the room where *I* was guvnor – because that's what I was at the housekeeper's. It may have been a smaller place than upstairs, but I was more comfy, and I wasn't pulled around and slobbered over by the children like upstairs. The food was just as good as before, and there was more of it! I had my own cushion, and there was a stove that was the best place in the world at times like this! I used to creep down under it so that I got black all over. Oh – I still dream about that stove. Grroff! Grroff!"

"Do stoves look as nice as all that?" asked the snowman. "Like me?"

"Like the opposite of you! It's coal black – it's got a long neck with a brass collar – and it eats fire-wood so that flames come out of its mouth. If you get down beside it or, better still, under it, then it's the most comfortable place in the world! You can see it through the window from where you're standing!"

And the snowman looked, and, sure enough he saw a black polished thing with a brass collar and flames flickering down below. The snowman came over all peculiar; he had a strange feeling that he couldn't put a name to; it wasn't anything he knew about – but most people will know it, provided they're not snowmen.

"And why did you leave her?" asked the snowman. (He felt that the stove must be some sort of woman.) "How could you leave such a lovely place?"

"I'd no choice," said the watchdog. "They threw me out and chained me up here. I'd bitten the youngest young master in the leg because he pinched the bone that I was gnawing. Well – 'bone for bone', says I, but they didn't like it, and from then on

I've been on this chain, and I've lost my nice voice. Just hear how hoarse I am: Grroff! Grroff! That's the finish of it."

But the snowman wasn't listening; he kept on looking into the house-keeper's room in the cellar where the stove stood on its four iron legs, the same height as the snowman himself.

"Everything's scrunching down inside me," he said. "Shall I ever get in there? It's an innocent enough wish, and innocent wishes must surely be granted. It's my highest wish, my very only wish, and it really wouldn't be fair for it not to be granted. I must

get in there, I must get beside her, even if I have to break a window."

"You'll never get in," said the watchdog, "and if you did reach the stove then you'd soon get off – grroff! grroff!"

"I'm as good as off," said the snowman, "I think I'm breaking up."

The snowman stood there for the whole day, looking through the window. As the light faded the room looked even more inviting. A gentle light came from the stove, not like the moon or the sun – no – it was like the light of a stove when it's got something inside it. When they opened its door flames leapt out as they always did. It made the snowman's white face red with blushes which went on half-way down his body.

"I can't take it," he said. "How beautiful she is with her tongue out!"

It was a long, long night – but not for the snowman. He was lost in his own beautiful thoughts and freezing till he crackled.

In the morning the cellar windows were frozen over with the most beautiful flowers of ice that any snowman could wish for – but they hid the stove. The ice wouldn't melt on the panes, so he couldn't see her. Everything crackled and crunched; it was just the kind of frosty weather that a snowman should enjoy – but he didn't enjoy it; he could – and really should – have felt so light-hearted – but he wasn't light-hearted. He was love-sick for the stove.

"That's a nasty complaint for a snowman," said the watchdog. "Mind you, I've had it myself, but I got over it. Grroff! Grroff! Now we'll get a shift in the weather."

And the weather did shift; it began to thaw. And the more the weather thawed, the more the snowman thawed too. But he didn't say anything; he didn't grizzle – and that's a sure sign . . .

One morning he collapsed. Where he stood something stuck up in the air like the handle of a broom, and that's what the boys had built him round.

"Now I can see why he was love-sick," said the watchdog. "The snowman had a stove-rake in his body, and that's what was making him so spoony – but now he's got over it. Grroff! Grroff!"

And soon they'd got over the weather too.

"Grroff! Grroff!" barked the watchdog – but the little girls on the farm sang:

> "Primrose, primrose
> Pretty face!
> Willow, willow
> Woolly lace!
> Lark and cuckoo
> Come and sing,
> February
> Heralds spring.
> Whistle, whistle
> Call – call –
> Come the sunshine
> Over all."

And nobody thought about the snowman.

A VISIT FROM ST. NICHOLAS

CLEMENT C. MOORE

'Twas the night before Christmas, when all
    through the house
Not a creature was stirring, not even a
    mouse;
The stockings were hung by the chimney
    with care,
In hopes that St. Nicholas soon would be
    there;
The children were nestled all snug in their
    beds,
While visions of sugar-plums danced in their
    heads;

And Mamma in her 'kerchief, and I in my
cap,
Had just settled our brains for a long winter's
nap;
When out on the lawn there arose such a
clatter,
I sprang from the bed to see what was the
matter.
Away to the window I flew like a flash,
Tore open the shutters and threw up the
sash.
The moon on the breast of the new-fallen
snow,
Gave the lustre of mid-day to objects below,
When, what to my wondering eyes should
appear,
But a miniature sleigh, and eight tiny
reindeer,
With a little old driver, so lively and quick,
I knew in a moment it must be St. Nick.

More rapid than eagles his coursers they
    came,
And he whistled, and shouted, and called
    them by name;

"Now, *Dasher!* now, *Dancer!* now, *Prancer*
    and *Vixen!*
On, *Comet!* on, *Cupid!* on, *Donner* and
    Blitzen!
To the top of the porch! to the top of the wall!
Now dash away! dash away! dash away all!"
As dry leaves that before the wild hurricane
    fly,
When they meet with an obstacle, mount to
    the sky;

So up to the house-top the coursers they
    flew,
With the sleigh full of toys, and St. Nicholas
    too.
And then in a twinkling, I heard on the roof,
The prancing and pawing of each little hoof—
As I drew in my head, and was turning
    around,
Down the chimney St. Nicholas came with a
    bound.

He was dressed all in fur, from his head to
    his foot,
And his clothes were all tarnished with ashes
    and soot;

A bundle of toys he had flung on his back,
And he looked like a pedlar just opening his
pack.

His eyes – how they twinkled! his dimples,
how merry!
His cheeks were like roses, his nose like a
cherry!

His droll little mouth was drawn up like a
bow,
And the beard of his chin was as white as the
snow;
The stump of a pipe he held tight in his
teeth,

And the smoke it encircled his head like a
wreath;
He had a broad face and a little round belly,
That shook when he laughed, like a bowlful
of jelly.

He was chubby and plump, a right jolly old
elf,
And I laughed when I saw him, in spite of
myself,
A wink of his eye and a twist of his head,
Soon gave me to know I had nothing to
dread;
He spoke not a word, but went straight to his
work,

And filled all the stockings; then turned with
   a jerk,
And laying his finger aside of his nose,
And giving a nod, up the chimney he rose;
He sprang to his sleigh, to his team gave a
   whistle,
And away they all flew like the down of a
   thistle.
But I heard him exclaim, ere he drove out of
   sight,

"HAPPY CHRISTMAS TO ALL AND
   TO ALL A GOOD NIGHT"

THE GIFT OF THE MAGI

O. HENRY

One dollar and eighty-seven cents. That was all. And sixty cents of it was in pennies. Pennies saved one and two at a time by bulldozing the grocer and the vegetable man and the butcher until one's cheeks burned with the silent imputation of parsimony that such close dealing implied. Three times Della counted it. One dollar and eighty-seven cents. And the next day would be Christmas.

There was clearly nothing to do but flop down on the shabby little couch and howl. So Della did it. Which instigates the moral reflection that life is made up of sobs, sniffles, and smiles, with sniffles predominating.

While the mistress of the home is gradually subsiding from the first stage to the second, take a look at the home. A furnished flat at $8 per week. It did not exactly beggar description, but it certainly had that word on the lookout for the mendicancy squad.

In the vestibule below was a letter-box into which no letter

would go, and an electric button from which no mortal finger could coax a ring. Also appertaining thereunto was a card bearing the name "Mr. James Dillingham Young."

The "Dillingham" had been flung to the breeze during a former period of prosperity when its possessor was being paid $30 per week. Now, when the income was shrunk to $20, the letters of "Dillingham" looked blurred, as though they were thinking seriously of contracting to a modest and unassuming D. But whenever Mr. James Dillingham Young came home and reached his flat above he was called "Jim" and greatly hugged by Mrs. James Dillingham Young, already introduced to you as Della. Which is all very good.

Della finished her cry and attended to her cheeks with the powder rag. She stood by the window and looked out dully at a grey cat walking a grey fence in a grey backyard. Tomorrow would be Christmas Day, and she had only $1.87 with which to buy Jim a present. She had been saving every penny she could for months, with this result. Twenty dollars a week doesn't go far. Expenses had been greater than she had calculated. They always are. Only $1.87 to buy a present for Jim. Her Jim. Many a happy hour she had spent planning for something nice for him. Something fine and rare and sterling – something just a little bit near to being worthy of the honour of being owned by Jim.

There was a pier-glass between the windows of the room. Perhaps you have seen a pier-glass in an $8 flat. A very thin and very agile person may, by observing his reflection in a rapid sequence of longitudinal strips, obtain a fairly accurate conception of his looks. Della, being slender, had mastered the art.

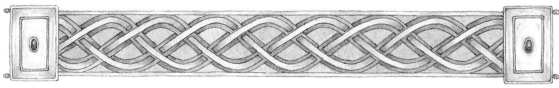

Suddenly she whirled from the window and stood before the glass. Her eyes were shining brilliantly, but her face had lost its colour within twenty seconds. Rapidly she pulled down her hair and let it fall to its full length.

Now, there were two possessions of the James Dillingham Youngs in which they both took a mighty pride. One was Jim's gold watch that had been his father's and his grandfather's. The other was Della's hair. Had the Queen of Sheba lived in the flat across the airshaft, Della would have let her hair hang out the window some day to dry just to depreciate Her Majesty's jewels and gifts. Had King Solomon been the janitor, with all his treasures piled up in the basement, Jim would have pulled out his watch every time he passed, just to see him pluck at his beard from envy.

So now Della's beautiful hair fell about her, rippling and shining like a cascade of brown waters. It reached below her knee and made itself almost a garment for her. And then she did it up again nervously and quickly. Once she faltered for a minute and stood still while a tear or two splashed on the worn red carpet.

On went her old brown jacket; on went her old brown hat. With a

whirl of skirts and with the brilliant sparkle still in her eyes, she fluttered out the door and down the stairs to the street.

Where she stopped the sign read: "Mme Sofronie. Hair Goods of All Kinds." One flight up Della ran, and collected herself, panting. Madame, large, too white, chilly, hardly looked the "Sofronie."

"Will you buy my hair?" asked Della.

"I buy hair," said Madame. "Take yer hat off and let's have a sight at the looks of it."

Down rippled the brown cascade.

"Twenty dollars," said Madame, lifting the mass with a practised hand.

"Give it to me quick," said Della.

Oh, and the next two hours tripped by on rosy wings. Forget the hashed metaphor. She was ransacking the stores for Jim's present.

She found it at last. It surely had been made for Jim and no one else. There was no other like it in any of the stores, and she had turned all of them inside out. It was a platinum fob chain simple and chaste in design, properly proclaiming its value by substance alone and not by meretricious ornamentation – as all good things should do. It was even worthy of The Watch. As soon as she saw it she knew that it must be Jim's. It was like him. Quietness and value

– the description applied to both. Twenty-one dollars they took from her for it, and she hurried home with the 87 cents. With that chain on his watch Jim might be properly anxious about the time in any company. Grand as the watch was, he sometimes looked at it on the sly on account of the old leather strap that he used in place of a chain.

When Della reached home her intoxication gave way a little to prudence and reason. She got out her curling irons and lighted the gas and went to work repairing the ravages made by generosity added to love. Which is always a tremendous task, dear friends – a mammoth task.

Within forty minutes her head was covered with tiny, close-lying curls that made her look wonderfully like a truant schoolboy. She looked at her reflection in the mirror long, carefully, and critically.

"If Jim doesn't kill me," she said to herself, "before he takes a second look at me, he'll say I look like a Coney Island chorus girl. But what could I do – oh! what could I do with a dollar and eighty-seven cents?"

At 7 o'clock the coffee was made and the frying-pan was on the back of the stove, hot and ready to cook the chops.

Jim was never late. Della doubled the fob chain in her hand and sat on the corner of the table near the door that he always entered. Then she heard his step on the stair away down on the first flight, and she turned white for just a moment. She had a habit of saying

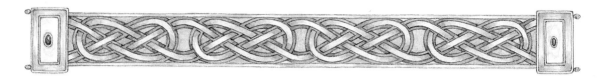

little silent prayers about the simplest everyday things, and now she whispered: "Please God, make him think I am still pretty."

The door opened and Jim stepped in and closed it. He looked thin and very serious. Poor fellow, he was only twenty-two – and to be burdened with a family! He needed a new overcoat and he was without gloves.

Jim stopped inside the door, as immovable as a setter at the scent of quail. His eyes were fixed upon Della, and there was an expression in them that she could not read, and it terrified her. It was not anger, nor surprise, nor disapproval, nor horror, nor any of the sentiments that she had been prepared for. He simply stared at her fixedly with that peculiar expression on his face.

Della wriggled off the table and went for him.

"Jim, darling," she cried, "don't look at me that way. I had my hair cut off and sold it because I couldn't have lived through Christmas without giving you a present. It'll grow out again – you won't mind, will you? I just had to do it. My hair grows awfully fast. Say 'Merry Christmas!' Jim, and let's be happy. You don't know what a nice – what a beautiful, nice gift I've got for you."

"You've cut off your hair?" asked Jim, laboriously, as if he had not arrived at that patent fact yet even after the hardest mental labour.

"Cut it off and sold it," said Della. "Don't you like me just as well, anyhow? I'm me without my hair, ain't I?"

Jim looked about the room curiously.

"You say your hair is gone?" he said, with an air almost of idiocy.

"You needn't look for it," said Della. "It's sold, I tell you – sold and gone, too. It's Christmas Eve, boy. Be good to me, for it went

for you. Maybe the hairs of my head were numbered," she went on with a sudden serious sweetness, "but nobody could ever count my love for you. Shall I put the chops on, Jim?"

Out of his trance Jim seemed quickly to wake. He enfolded his Della. For ten seconds let us regard with discreet scrutiny some inconsequential object in the other direction. Eight dollars a week or a million a year – what is the difference? A mathematician or a wit would give you the wrong answer. The magi brought valuable gifts, but that was not among them. This dark assertion will be illuminated later on.

Jim drew a package from his overcoat pocket and threw it upon the table.

"Don't make any mistake, Dell," he said, "about me. I don't think there's anything in the way of a haircut or a shave or a shampoo that could make me like my girl any less. But if you'll unwrap that package you may see why you had me going a while at first."

White fingers and nimble tore at the string and paper. And then an ecstatic scream of joy; and then, alas! a quick feminine change to hysterical tears and wails, necessitating the immediate employment of all the comforting powers of the lord of the flat.

For there lay The Combs – the set of combs, side and back, that

Della had worshipped for long in a Broadway window. Beautiful combs, pure tortoise shell, with jewelled rims – just the shade to wear in the beautiful vanished hair. They were expensive combs, she knew, and her heart had simply craved and yearned over them without the least hope of possession. And now, they were hers, but the tresses that should have adorned the coveted adornments were gone.

But she hugged them to her bosom, and at length she was able to look up with dim eyes and a smile and say: "My hair grows so fast, Jim!"

And then Della leaped up like a little singed cat and cried, "Oh, oh!"

Jim had not yet seen his beautiful present. She held it out to him eagerly upon her open palm. The dull precious metal seemed to flash with a reflection of her bright and ardent spirit.

"Isn't it a dandy, Jim? I hunted all over town to find it. You'll have to look at the time a hundred times a day now. Give me your watch. I want to see how it looks on it."

Instead of obeying, Jim tumbled down on the couch and put his hands under the back of his head and smiled.

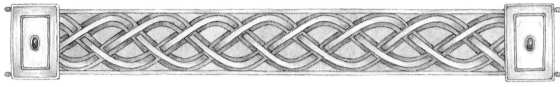

"Dell," said he, "let's put our Christmas presents away and keep 'em a while. They're too nice to use just at present. I sold the watch to get the money to buy your combs. And now suppose you put the chops on."

The magi, as you know, were wise men – wonderfully wise men – who brought gifts to the Babe in the manger. They invented the art of giving Christmas presents. Being wise, their gifts were no doubt wise ones, possibly bearing the privilege of exchange in case of duplication. And here I have lamely related to you the uneventful chronicle of two foolish children in a flat who most unwisely sacrificed for each other the greatest treasures of their house. But in a last word to the wise of these days let it be said that of all who give gifts these two were the wisest. Of all who give and receive gifts, such as they are wisest. Everywhere they are wisest. They are the magi.

WE THREE KINGS
OF ORIENT ARE

JOHN HENRY HOPKINS

We three Kings of Orient are,
Bearing gifts we travel so far,
Field and fountain, moor and mountain,
Following yonder star.

O star of wonder, star of night,
Star with royal beauty bright,
Westward leading, still proceeding,
Guide us to thy perfect light.

Born a King on Bethlehem's plain,
Gold I bring, to crown him again,
King for ever, ceasing never,
Over us all to reign.

Frankincense to offer have I,
Incense owns a Deity nigh.
Prayer and praising, all men raising
Worshipping God most high.

Myrrh is mine, its bitter perfume
Breathes a life of gathering gloom;
Sorrowing, sighing, bleeding, dying,
Sealed in the stone-cold tomb.

Glorious now behold him arise,
King and God and sacrifice,
Alleluia, Alleluia;
Earth to the heavens replies.

O star of wonder, star of night,
Star with royal beauty bright,
Westward leading, still proceeding,
Guide us to thy perfect light.

BERTIE'S ESCAPADE

KENNETH GRAHAME

I

It was eleven o'clock on a winter's night. The fields, the hedges, the trees, were white with snow. From over Quarry Woods floated the sound of Marlow bells, practising for Christmas. In the paddock the only black spot visible was Bertie's sty, and the only thing blacker than the sty was Bertie himself, sitting in the front courtyard and yawning. In Mayfield windows the lights were out, and the whole house was sunk in slumber.

"This is very slow," yawned Bertie. "Why I shouldn't I *do* something?"

Bertie was a pig of action. "Deeds, not grunts," was his motto. Retreating as far back as he could, he took a sharp run, gave a mighty jump, and cleared his palings.

"The rabbits shall come too," he said. "Do them good."

He went to the rabbit-hutch, and unfastened the door. "Peter! Benjie!" he called. "Wake up!"

"Whatever are you up to, Bertie?" said Peter sleepily.

"Come on!" said Bertie. "We're going carol-singing. Bring Benjie too, and hurry up!"

Peter hopped out at once, in great delight. But Benjie grumbled, and burrowed down in his straw. So they hauled him out by his ears.

Cautiously they crept down the paddock, past the house, and out

at the front gate. Down the hill they went, took the turning by the pillar-box, and arrived at the foot of Chalkpit Hill. Then Benjie struck.

"Hang it all," he said. "I'm not going to fag up that hill tonight for any one!"

"Then I'll bite you," said Bertie. "Choose which you please."

"It's all right, Bertie," said Peter. "We're none of us going to fag up that hill. I know an easier way. You follow me."

He led them into the chalk-pit, till they stood at the very foot. Looking up, it was like the cliffs at Broadstairs, only there was no band at the top and no bathing-machines at the bottom.

Peter pulled out a large lump of chalk and disclosed the entrance to a long dark little tunnel. "Come on!" he said, and dived in; and the others followed.

II

They groped along the tunnel for a considerable way in darkness and silence, till at last they saw a glimmer of light; and presently the

tunnel ended suddenly in a neat little lift, lit up with electric light, with a seat running round three sides of it. A mole was standing by the door.

"Come along there, please, if you're going up!" called the mole sharply.

They hurried in and sat down. "Just in time!" said Peter.

"Any more for the lift?" cried the mole, looking down the tunnel. Then he stepped inside smartly, slammed the door, pulled the rope, and they shot upwards.

"Well, I never!" gasped Bertie. "Peter, you do know a thing or two, you do! Where – what – how – "

The lift stopped with a jerk. The mole flung the door open, saying, "Pass out quickly, please!" and slammed it behind them. They found themselves standing on the fresh snow, under the open starlit sky.

They turned round to ask the mole where they were, but the lift had vanished. Where it had been there was a square patch of grass free from snow, and in the middle of the patch was a buttony white mushroom.

"Why, we're in Spring Lane!" cried Bertie. "There's the well!"

"And here's Mr. Stone's lodge, just in front of us!" cried Peter.

"Splendid!" said Bertie. "Now, we'll go right up to the house, and sing our bewitching carols under the drawing-room windows. And presently, Mr. Stone will come out, and praise us, and pat our heads, and say we're dern clever animals, and ask us in. And that will mean supper in the dining-room, and champagne with it, and grand times!"

They hurried up the drive, and planted themselves under the windows. Then Bertie said, "First we'll give 'em 'Good King Wenceslas'. Now then, all together!"

"But I don't know 'Good King Wenceslas'," said Peter.

"And I can't sing!" said Benjie.

"Well, you must both do the best you can," said Bertie. "Try and follow me. I'll sing very slow." And he struck up.

Peter followed him, as best he could, about two bars behind; and Benjie, who could not sing, imitated various musical instruments, not very successfully.

Presently they heard a voice, inside the house. It was Mrs. Stone's, and she was saying "What – on – earth – is – that – horrible caterwauling?"

Then they heard another voice – Mr. Stone's – replying: "It sounds like animals – horrid little animals – under the windows, squealing and grunting. I will go out with a big stick, and drive them away."

"Stick! O my!" said Bertie.

"Stick! Ow, ow!" said Benjie.

Then they heard Mrs. Stone again, saying, "O no, don't trouble to go out, dear. Go through the stable yard to the kennels, and LET – LOOSE – ALL – THE – DOGS."

III

"Dogs, O my!" said Bertie.

"Dogs, ow, ow!" said Benjie.

They turned tail and ran for their lives. Peter had already started, some ten seconds previously; they saw him sprinting down the carriage-drive ahead of them, a streak of rabbit-skin. Bertie ran and ran, and Benjie ran and ran; while behind them, and coming nearer and nearer, they could hear plainly

Wow – wow – wow – wow – wow – WOW!

Peter was the first to reach the mushroom. He flung himself on it and pressed it; and, click! the little lift was there! The door was flung open, and the mole, stepping out, said sharply: "Now then! hurry up, please, if you're going down! Any more for the lift?"

Hurry up indeed! There was no need to say that. They flung themselves on the seat, breathless and exhausted; the mole slammed the door and pulled the rope, and they sank downwards.

Then the mole looked them over and grinned. "Had a pleasant evening?" he inquired.

Bertie would not answer, he was too sulky; but Peter replied sarcastically: "O yes, first rate. My friend here's a popular carol singer. They make him welcome wherever he goes, and give him the best of everything."

"Now don't you start pulling my leg, Peter," said Bertie, "for I won't stand it. I've been a failure tonight, and I admit it; and I'll tell you what I will do to make up for it. You two come back to my sty, and I'll give you a first-rate supper, the best you ever had!"

"O ah, first-rate cabbage-stalks," said Benjie. "*We* know your suppers!"

"Not at all," said Bertie earnestly. "On the contrary. There's a window in Mayfield that I can get into the house by, at any time. And I know where Mr. Grahame keeps his keys – very careless man, Mr. Grahame. Put your trust in me, and you shall have cold chicken, tongue, pressed beef, jellies, trifle, *and* champagne – at least; perhaps more, but that's the least you'll have!"

Here the lift stopped with a jerk. "Tumble out, all of you," said the mole, flinging the door open. "And look sharp, for it's closing time, and I'm going home."

"No you're not, old man," said Bertie affectionately. "You're coming along to have supper with us."

The mole protested it was much too late; but in the end they persuaded him.

IV

When they got back to Mayfield, the rabbits took the mole off to wash his hands and brush his hair; while Bertie disappeared cautiously round a corner of the house. In about ten minutes he appeared at the pigsty, staggering under the weight of two large baskets. One of them contained all the eatables he had already mentioned, as well as apples, oranges, chocolates, ginger, and crackers. The other contained ginger-beer, soda-water, and champagne.

The supper was laid in the inner pigsty. They were all very

hungry, naturally; and when everything was ready they sat down, and stuffed, and drank, and told stories, and all talked at once; and when they had stuffed enough, they proposed toasts, and drank healths – ."The King" – "Our host Bertie" – "Mr. Grahame" – "The Visitors, coupled with the name of Mole" – "Absent friends, coupled with the name of Mr. Stone" – and many others. Then there were speeches, and songs, and then more speeches, and more songs; and it was three o'clock in the morning before the mole slipped through the palings and made his way back to his own home, where Mrs. Mole was sitting up for him, in some uneasiness of mind.

Mr. Grahame's night was a very disturbed one, owing to agitating dreams. He dreamt that the house was broken into by burglars, and he wanted to get up and go down and catch them, but he could not move hand or foot. He heard them ransacking his pantry, stealing his cold chicken and things, and plundering his wine-cellar, and still he could not move a muscle. Then he dreamt that he was at one

of the great City Banquets that he used to go to, and he heard the Chairman propose the health of "The King" and there was great cheering. And he thought of a most excellent speech to make in reply – a really clever speech. And he tried to make it, but they held him down in his chair and wouldn't let him. And then he dreamt that the Chairman actually proposed his own health – the health of Mr. Grahame! and he got up to reply, and he couldn't think of anything to say! And so he stood there, for hours and hours it seemed, in a dead silence, the glittering eyes of the guests – there were hundreds and hundreds of guests – all fixed on him, and still he couldn't think of anything to say! Till at last the Chairman rose, and said "He can't think of anything to say! *Turn him out!*" Then the waiters fell upon him, and dragged him from the room, and threw him into the street, and flung his hat and coat after him; and as he was shot out he heard the whole company singing wildly "For he's a jolly good fellow – !"

He woke up in a cold perspiration. And then a strange thing happened. Although he was awake – he knew he was awake – he could distinctly hear shrill little voices, still singing "For he's a jolly good fe-e-llow, and so say all of us!" He puzzled over it for a few minutes, and then, fortunately, he fell asleep.

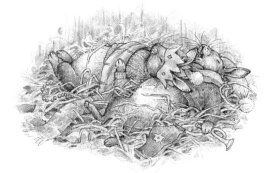

Next morning, when Miss S. and A.G. went to call on the rabbits, they found a disgraceful state of things. The hutch in a most untidy mess, clothes flung about anyhow, and Peter and Benjie sprawling on the floor, fast asleep and snoring frightfully. They tried to wake them, but the rabbits only murmured something about "jolly good fellows," and fell asleep again.

"Well, we never!" said Miss S. and A.G..

When Albert King went to take Bertie his dinner, you cannot imagine the state he found the pigsty in. Such a litter of things of every sort, and Bertie in the midst of it all, fast asleep. King poked him with a stick, and said, "Dinner, Bertie!" But even then he didn't wake. He only grunted something that sounded like " – God – save – King – Wenceslas!"

"*Well!*" said King. "Of all the animals!"

LITTLE TREE

E.E. CUMMINGS

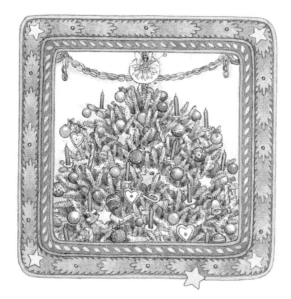

little tree
little silent Christmas tree
you are so little
you are more like a flower

who found you in the green forest
and were you very sorry to come away?
see   i will comfort you
because you smell so sweetly

i will kiss your cool bark
and hug you safe and tight
just as your mother would,
only don't be afraid

look   the spangles
that sleep all the year in a dark box
dreaming of being taken out and allowed to shine,
the balls the chains red and gold the fluffy threads,

put up your little arms
and i'll give them all to you to hold
every finger shall have its ring
and there won't be a single place dark or unhappy

then when you're quite dressed
you'll stand in the window for everyone to see
and how they'll stare!
oh but you'll be very proud

and my little sister and i will take hands
and looking up at our beautiful tree
we'll dance and sing
"Noel Noel"

A CHRISTMAS TREE FOR LYDIA

ELIZABETH ENRIGHT

Lydia first learned about Christmas when she was one year old. Draped over her mother's shoulder she drooled and stared, and the lights of the Christmas tree made other lights in her large tranced eyes and in the glaze of spittle on her chin.

When she was two years old she learned about Santa Claus. She paid very little attention to him then, but when she was three she talked about him a lot and they had some difficulty persuading her that he and the infant Jesus were not father and son. By the time she was four she had come to accept him as one of the ordered

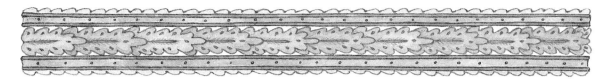

phenomena that ruled her life, like daytime and nighttime: one seven o'clock for getting up and another seven o'clock for going to bed. Like praise and blame and winter and summer and her brother's right of seniority and her mother's last word. Her father did not exist in her field of magnitudes; he had been killed in Cassino the winter she was born.

"Santa Claus will come," Lydia said, and knew it was as true as saying tomorrow will come. "He will bring a Christmas tree. Big. With lights. With colours."

When she was four, her brother Eddy was nine and had long ago found out the truth concerning the matter. No note of illusion deceived his eye when he passed the street-corner Santas at Christmas time, standing beside their imitation chimneys, ringing their bells; he saw them for what they were. He saw how all their trousers bagged and their sleeves were too long, and how, above the false beards tied loosely on like bibs, their noses ran and their eyes looked out, mortal and melancholy.

"You'd think the kid would catch on," Eddy said to his mother. "Gee, when you notice the differentness of them all."

Lydia believed in every one of them, from the bell-ringers on the street corners to the department-store variety who always asked the same questions and whose hired joviality grew glassy towards evening. She had faith in the monster idol in the store on

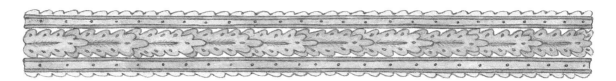

Fourteenth Street which turned its glaring face from side to side and laughed a huge stony machinery laugh all day long, filling the region with sounds of compulsive derangement. For Lydia, the saint was ubiquitous, ingenious, capable of all, and looking into the different faces of his impersonators she beheld the one good face she had invented for him.

"Eddy, don't you tell her now, will you?" his mother said. "Don't you dare to, now. Remember she's only four."

Sure, let the kid have her fun, thought Eddy, with large scorn and slight compassion. He himself remembered long-ago Christmas Eves when he had listened for bells in the air, and watched the limp shape of his sock hung up over the stove.

"How can he come in through the *stove*, Mum?"

"In houses like this he comes in through the window. Go to sleep now, Eddy, like a good boy."

Eddy went to public school in the daytimes and Lydia went to a

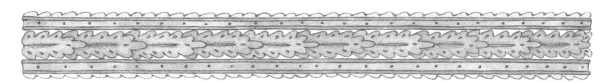

day nursery. Her mother called for her every evening on the way home from work. She was a thin dark young woman whose prettiness was often obscured by the ragged shadows of irritation and fatigue. She loved her children, but worry gnawed at her relations with them, sharpening her words and shortening her temper. Coming home in the evening, climbing up the stairs to the flat with one hand pressing the bags of groceries to her chest, and Lydia loitering and babbling, dragging on her other hand, she wished sometimes to let go of everything. To let go of Lydia, perhaps forever; to let go once and for all of the heavy paper grocery bags. It would be a savage happiness, she felt, to see and hear the catsup bottle smashed on the stairs, the eggs broken and leaking, and all the tin cans and potatoes rolling and banging their way downward.

They lived in a two-room flat with linoleum on the floor and a lively corrugated ceiling. In the daytime, from noon on, the rooms were hot with sunshine, but in the morning and at night they were as cold as caves unless the stove was going. The stove and the bathtub and the sink were all in the front room where Eddy slept.

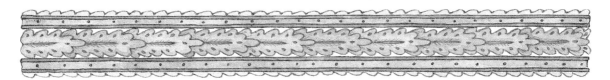

Sometimes at night the bathtub would gulp lonesomely, and the leaky tap of the sink had a drip as perfect in tempo as a clock.

Lydia and her mother slept in the back room, a darkish place, painted blue, with a big dim mirror over the bureau, and a window looking on to a shaft. The toilet was by itself in a little cubicle with a window also looking on to the shaft. When the chain was pulled it was as though one had released a river genie; a great storming and rumbling rose upward through the pipes, shaking all the furniture in the flat, then there was a prolonged crashing of waters lasting for minutes, and at last the mighty withdrawal, thundering and wrathful, growing fainter at last, and still fainter, till silence was restored, docile and appeased.

Sometimes when Eddy was alone and the stillness got to be too much for him he went into the water closet and pulled the chain just for the company of the noise.

He was often alone during the first part of his vacation. At noon,

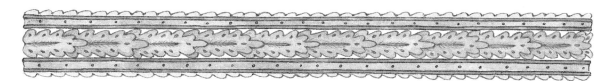

wearing his blue and grey Mackinaw and his aviator's helmet with the straps flying, he came stamping up the stairs and into the sun-flooded crowded little flat. Humming and snuffling, he made his lunch: breakfast food, or huge erratic sandwiches filled with curious materials. When he was through he always cleaned up: washed the bowl or dish and swept up the breadcrumbs with his chapped hand. He had learned to be tidy at an early age, and could even make his bed well enough to sleep in it.

In the afternoons and mornings he voyaged forth with Joey Camarda, and others, to the street for contests of skill and wit. Sometimes they went to the upper reaches of the park with its lakes, bridges, battlegrounds and ambushes. Or rainy days they tagged through the museums, shrill and shabby as sparrows, touching the raddled surfaces of meteorites without awe, and tipping back their heads boldly to stare at the furious mask of Tyrannosaurus Rex.

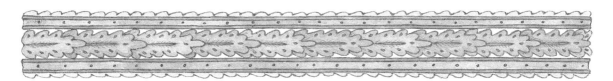

"He isn't real. They made him out of pieces of wood, like," Joey said. "Men with ladders made him."

"He is, too, real," Eddy said. "He walked around and ate and growled and everything. Once he did."

"Naw, he wasn't real. Jeez he *couldn't* be real. You'd believe anything. You'd believe in Santy Claus even."

Christmas and its symbols were more and more in their conversation as the time drew near. They speculated on the subject of possible gifts to themselves. Joey said his uncle was going to give him roller skates and a real Mauser rifle.

"It's one he got when he was in It'ly. What are you going to get, Eddy?"

Eddy said he thought he'd probably get a bike. It was just as likely that he would be given a bike as that he would be given the new moon out of the sky, but having made the statement, he went on to perfect it. He said that it would be a white bike with red trimming

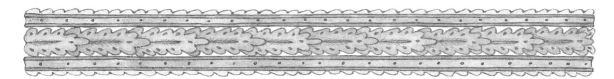

and a red piece of glass like a jewel on the back of it, and two raccoon tails floating from the handle bars.

"There's going to be two kinds of bells on the handle bars. One will be kind of a si-reen."

"Will you let me ride on it sometimes, Ed?"

"Sometimes," Eddy said.

That night he rode the bike all around the flat with the raccoon tails lying out on the speed-torn air. The tail-light blazed like a red-hot ruby, and the siren was as terrible as human voice could make it.

"Watch me now, I'm taking a curve," shouted Eddy. "Eee-ow-oooo-eee. Just missed that truck by half an inch!"

Lydia sat safely on the bed in the back room questioning him as he flashed by.

"Is it a plane, Eddy?"

"No."

"Is it a car?"

"No."

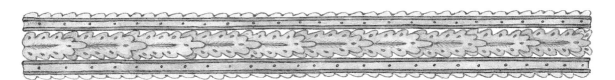

"Is it a – is it a train?"

"No. Gosh, it's a bike. Look out now. I got to make that light. Eee-ow-ooo-eee!"

"Eddy, will you please for pity's sake *shut up*!" cried his mother. "I can't hear myself think, even!"

He came to a stop. "Gee, Mum, what are you cross about?"

She didn't look at him; she pushed the potatoes and onions around the frying pan with a fork. Then she shook salt over them, and spoke from a certain distance.

"Eddy, you kids don't get a tree this year."

"Heck, why not? What did we do? Why not?"

"I can't afford it, that's why!" she cried loudly, angry with him because she was hurting him. Then she lowered her voice. "They don't want me back at the store after Christmas, they told me today. They don't need me any more. I don't dare to get you any presents even but just things you have to have like socks and mittens." She looked at him. "Maybe some candy," she added.

A stinging hot odour arose from the frying pan to join the robust company of cooking smells from other flats on other floors: herring and chili and garlic and pork.

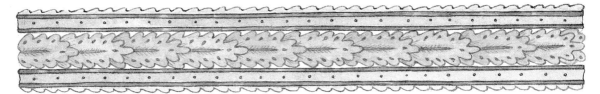

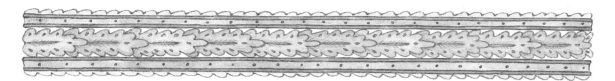

"Gee, Eddy, I'm scared to spend another cent. How do I know I'll get another job?"

"What are you going to tell Lydia? She talks about the Christmas tree all day long."

"She'll have to do without, that's all. Other people have to do without."

"But, gee, she talks about it all day long."

His mother threw down the fork and whirled on him.

"I can't *help* it, can I? My God, what am *I* supposed to do?"

Eddy knew better than to go on with it. He leaned against the sink and thought, and when they ate supper he was kind and forbearing with Lydia who was both hilarious and sloppy. After a while his kindness became preoccupied, like that of one who drinks secretly at a spring of inspiration, and when Lydia had gone to bed he made a suggestion to his mother.

"I have an idea. If we put Christmas off for a few days, maybe a week, I can fix everything."

His mother, as he had expected, said no. It was this response on the part of his mother which was the starting point of all his campaigns, many of them successful. He leaned against the sink and waited.

"What good would it do? And anyway what would Lydia think!" she said.

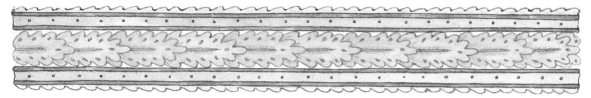

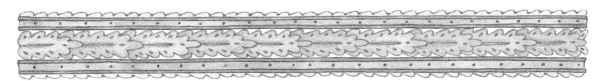

"Tell her Santa Claus is late. Tell her we made a mistake about the day. She's too dumb to know the difference. Everyone's dumb when they're four."

"And anyway it seems kind of wrong."

"What would Jesus care if we put his birthday off for a couple of days?"

"Oh, Eddy, don't be silly. There won't be any more money than there is now."

"No, but I got an idea. Please, Mum, please. Please."

Eddy knew how to pester nicely. He had a quiet attentive way of looking and looking at one; of following one with his eyes and not saying anything, the request still shimmering all around him like heat-lightning. He waited.

His mother hung up the wet dishtowel and turned the dishpan upside down. She looked into the little mirror above the sink and looked away again. Then she sat down in the rocker and opened

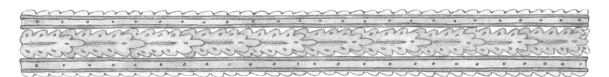

the tabloid newspaper.

"Oh, all *right*," she said. "For pity's sake, Eddy. What do you expect, a miracle?"

"Isn't there ever any miracles? Anyway I'm not thinking about a miracle, I'm thinking about something smart," Eddy said.

Christmas came, and for them it was a day like any other, except that their mother was at home. But it was easy to explain to Lydia that this was because her job at the store had ended for good, just as it was easy to explain Lydia's own absence from nursery school by the simple method of rubbing Vick's ointment on her chest. Eddy thought of that one, too.

"Gee, Eddy, I hope you know what you're doing," his mother said.

"I do know," Eddy said.

"You should at least tell *me* what you're going to do."

"It has to be a surprise for you, too," Eddy said, not so much because he wanted to surprise his mother as because he knew if he

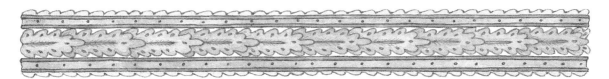

revealed his plan he would come in contact with a "no" which none of his stratagems could dissolve.

"It will be okay, Mum."

"And when is it to be, if I may ask?"

"On New Year's Day, I guess," Eddy said, and went in search of Joey Camarda whose help he had enlisted.

On New Year's Eve, early, he shut Lydia and his mother into their room.

"No matter what noises you hear, you don't come out, see? Promise."

"But, Eddy, I don't think – "

"You promise."

"Well – " his mother conceded, and that was as good as promising. She went in and shut the door, and before the extraordinary sounds of toil and shuffling commenced in the hall she was lost in the deep sleep of the discouraged: that temporary death

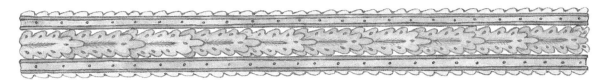

which is free from all the images of fear or joy.

At midnight the city woke up and met the New Year with a mighty purring. In the streets people blew horns and shook things that sounded like tin cans full of pebbles. Lydia woke up too and thought that it was Santa Claus.

"I wanna get up, Mum. I wanna see him."

"You lay down this minute or he won't leave a single thing. He doesn't like for people to be awake when he comes," said her mother crossly, clinging to the warm webs of sleep.

But Lydia sat up for a while in her cot, rocking softly to and fro. Through the crack under the door came a fragrance she remembered well from Christmas a year ago, and the Christmas before that.

In the morning it was a long time before Eddy would let them out of their room.

"Eddy, it's cold in here," said his mother.

"I wanna see the tree, I wanna see the tree," chanted Lydia, half singing, half whining. "I wanna see the tree, I wanna see the tree."

"Heck, wait a minute," said Eddy.

"I wanna see the tree, I wanna see the tree," bayed Lydia.

There were sounds of haste and struggle in the next room.

"All right, you can come in now," said Eddy, and opened the door.

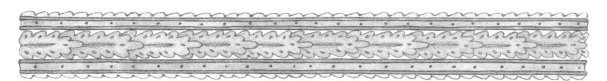

They saw a forest.

In a circle, hiding every wall, stood the Christmas trees; spare ones and stout ones, tall ones and short ones, but all tall to Lydia. Some still were hung with threads of silver foil, and here and there among the boughs the ornaments for a single tree had been distributed with justice; calm and bright as planets they turned and burned among the needles. The family stood in a mysterious grove, without bird or breeze, and there was a deep fragrance in the room. It was a smell of health and stillness and tranquillity, and for a minute or two, before she had thought of the dropping needles and the general inconvenience of a forest in the kitchen, Eddy's mother breathed the smell full into her city lungs and felt within herself a lessening of strain.

"Eddy, Eddy, how? How?"

"Me and Joe Camarda," Eddy whispered. "We went all around last night and dragged them out of gutters. We could of filled the

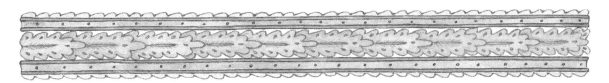

whole entire house with them if we wanted to. Last night in here it was like camping out."

It had been like that. He had lain peacefully in his bed under the branches, listening to the occasional snow-flake tinkle of a falling needle, and to the ticking of the leaky tap, hidden now as any forest spring.

"Eddy, honey, look at Lydia."

Lydia still looked new from her sleep. She stood in her flannel nightgown with her dark hair rumpled and her eyes full of lights, and her hands clasped in front of her in a composed, elderly way. Naturally a loud exuberant girl, the noise had temporarily been knocked out of her.

"All the Christmas trees," she remarked gently.

"Gee," said Eddy. "Don't get the idea it's going to be this way every year. This is just because he was late, and it's instead of presents."

It was enough for Lydia, anyone could see that. In a way, it was enough for Eddy too. He felt proud, generous and efficient. He felt successful. With his hands in his pockets he stood looking at his sister.

"All the Christmas trees," Lydia said quietly, and sighed. "All the Christmas trees."

A CHRISTMAS CAROL

CHRISTINA ROSSETTI

In the bleak mid-winter
   Frosty wind made moan,
Earth stood hard as iron,
   Water like a stone;
Snow had fallen, snow on snow,
   Snow on snow,
In the bleak mid-winter
   Long ago.

Our God, Heaven cannot hold Him
   Nor earth sustain;
Heaven and earth shall flee away
   When He comes to reign:
In the bleak mid-winter
   A stable-place sufficed
The Lord God Almighty
   Jesus Christ.

Enough for Him, whom cherubim
　　Worship night and day,
A breastful of milk
　　And a mangerful of hay;
Enough for Him, whom angels
　　Fall down before,
The ox and ass and camel
　　Which adore.

Angels and archangels
　　May have gathered there,
Cherubim and seraphim
　　Thronged the air;
But only His mother
　　In her maiden bliss
Worshipped the Beloved
　　With a kiss.

What can I give Him
　　Poor as I am?
If I were a shepherd
　　I would bring a lamb,
If I were a Wise Man
　　I would do my part, –
Yet what I can I give Him,
　　Give my heart.

THE OXEN

THOMAS HARDY

Christmas Eve, and twelve of the clock.
  "Now they are all on their knees,"
An elder said as we sat in a flock
  By the embers in hearthside ease.

We pictured the meek mild creatures where
  They dwelt in their strawy pen,
Nor did it occur to one of us there
  To doubt they were kneeling then.

So fair a fancy few would weave
  In these years! Yet, I feel,
If someone said on Christmas Eve,
  "Come; see the oxen kneel

"In the lonely barton by yonder coomb
  Our childhood used to know,"
I should go with him in the gloom,
  Hoping it might be so.

CHRISTMAS DAY

ALISON UTTLEY

from *A Country Child*

Susan awoke in the dark of Christmas morning. A weight lay on her feet, and she moved her toes up and down. She sat up and rubbed her eyes. It was Christmas Day. She stretched out her hands and found the knobby little stocking, which she brought into bed with her and clasped tightly in her arms as she fell asleep again.

She awoke later and lay holding her happiness, enjoying the moment. The light was dim, but the heavy mass of the chest of drawers stood out against the pale walls, all blue like the snowy shadows outside. She drew her curtains and looked out at the starry sky. She listened for the bells of the sleigh, but no sound came through the stillness except the screech owl's call.

Again she hadn't caught Santa Claus. Of course she knew he wasn't real, but also she knew he was. It was the same with everything. People said things were not alive but you knew in your heart they were: statues which would would catch you if you turned your back were made of stone; Santa Claus was your own father and mother; the stuffed fox died long ago.

But suppose people didn't *know*! They hadn't seen that stone woman walk in Broomy Vale Arboretum, but she might, in the dark

night. They hadn't seen Santa Claus and his sleigh, but that was because they were not quick enough. Susan had nearly caught things happening herself, she knew they only waited for her to go away. When she looked through a window into an empty room, there was always a guilty look about it, a stir of surprise.

Perhaps Santa Claus had left the marks of his reindeer and the wheels of his sleigh on the snow at the front of the house. She had never looked because last year there was no snow, and the year before she had believed in him absolutely. She would go out before breakfast, and perhaps she would find two marks of runners and a crowd of little hoofmarks.

She pinched the stocking from the toe to the top, where her white suspender tapes were stitched. It was full of nice knobs and lumps, and a flat thing like a book stuck out of the top. She drew it out – it *was* a book, just what she wanted most. She sniffed at it, and liked the smell of the cardboard back with deep letters cut in it. She ran her fingers along like a blind man and could not read the title, but there were three words in it.

Next came an apple, with its sweet, sharp odour. She recognized it, a yellow one, from the apple chamber, and from her favourite tree. She took a bite with her strong, white little teeth and scrunched it in the dark.

It was delicious fun, all alone, in this box-like room, with the dim blue-and-white jug on the washstand watching her, and the pool of the round mirror hanging on the wall, reflecting the blue dark outside, and the texts, "Thou God seest Me," and "Blessed are the Peacemakers," and "Though your sins be as scarlet they shall be white as wool." They could all see the things although she couldn't, and they were glad.

Next came a curious thing, pointed and spiked, with battlements like a tower. Whatever could it be? It was smooth like ivory and shone even in the dark. She ran her fingers round the little rim and found a knob. She gave it a tug, and a ribbon flew out – it was a tape-measure to measure a thousand things, the trees' girths, the calf's nose, the pony's tail. She put it on her knee and continued her search.

There was a tin ball that unscrewed and was filled with comfits, and an orange, and a sugar mouse, all these were easy to feel, a sugar watch with a paper face and a chain of coloured ribbon, a doll's chair, and a penny china doll with a round smooth head. She at once named it Diana, after Diana of the Ephesians, for this one could never be an idol, being made of pot. She put her next to her skin down the neck of her nightdress, and pulled the last little bumps out of the stocking toe. They were walnuts, smelling of the orchards at Bird-in-Bush Farm, where they grew on great trees overhanging the wall, and a silver shilling, the only one she ever got, and very great wealth, but it was intended for the money-box in the hall. It was the nicest Christmas stocking she had ever had, and she hugged her knees up to her chin and rocked with joy. Then she put her hand under her pillow and brought out five parcels which

had made five separate lumps under her head. They were quite safe.

She heard the alarm go off in her father's room and Dan's bell go jingle-jangle. Five o'clock, plenty of time yet before the hoof-marks would disappear. The wind swished softly against the window, and thumps and thuds sounded on the stairs. She slept again with the doll on her heart and the tape-measure under her cheek and the book in her hand.

She was awakened again by the rattle of milk-cans below her window. Joshua and Becky were coming back with the milk, and it really was Christmas Day. All else was strangely silent, for the deep snow deadened the sound of footsteps. She jumped out of bed, pressed her nose against the window, and rubbed away the Jack Frost pictures. Everything was blue, and a bright star shone. From a window in the farm buildings a warm gleam fell on the snow. Dan was milking the last cow by the light of the lantern which hung on the wall.

Then she heard his cheerful whistle and the low moo of the cows as he came out with the can.

What had the cattle done all night? Did they know it was Christmas? Of course, all God's creatures knew. Becky said the cows and horses knelt down on Christmas Eve. She could see them

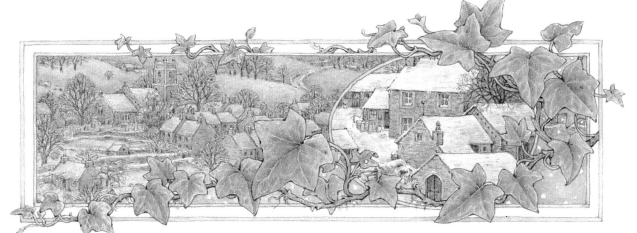

going down on their front knees, the cows so easily, the horses so painfully, for their legs were wrong. Sheep knelt when they had foot-rot, it would be easy for them. But down they all went, bowing to the New Saviour as she bowed to the new moon.

She washed in the basin with blue daisies round the rim, but she could see neither water nor soap. Candles were for night, not morning use. She brushed her hair in front of the ghost of a mirror, where a white little face looked like a flower-in-the-night. She slipped the round comb through her hair and put on her Sunday honey-combed dress with seven tucks in the skirt and two in the sleeves, a preparation for a long and lanky Susan.

Then she buttoned her slippers and said her short morning prayer, and down she tripped with her stocking-load of presents and the five parcels. She walked boldly past the fox and went to the landing window that overlooked the grass plots and lawn. The beeches were still, the apple trees stood blue and cream against the white hills, and there was a thin moon like a cow's horn in the trees.

She went into the hall and turned away from the closed kitchen door, where all was bustle, the noise of milk-cans, the roar of the fire, and the chatter of voices. The front door was unlocked and she

lifted the heavy iron catch and slipped out into the virgin snow, blue and strange in the early light.

She lifted her feet high and walked to the gate in the wall surrounding the house. The monkey tree held out its arms to her, and she waved a hand. She crossed the walk and looked over the low stone wall at the lawn. There was no doubt something had been there in the night, footprints, but not hoof-marks, a fox, maybe, or a dog visiting Roger.

She returned to the house, shivering with delight, and opened the kitchen door. She was wrapped in colour and light, in sweet smells of cows and hay and coldness, brought in by the men, and new milk and hot sausages, tea and toast, warmth and burning wood from the hearth. The strongest smell was cold, which rushed through the back door sweeping all the other smells away, until the doors banged and the flame of the fire shot out.

"A merry Christmas, a merry Christmas," she called, kissing everybody except Dan, which wouldn't be proper. "Merry" was the word Susan liked, not the limp word, "happy."

She presented her paper parcels all round and sat down on the settle to watch the different faces. Dan opened his quickly in the passage and took out a pencil. He licked the point, wrote on the back of his hairy hand, stuck it behind his ear, and grinned his thanks as he went off with his churn.

Becky had a pen-wiper, made out of a wishing-bone and a piece of Margaret's black skirt, and a quill pen cut from a goose feather.

"Just what I wanted," she cried nobly, for she didn't write a letter once a year, the reason being that she couldn't.

Old Joshua had a tiny bottle of scent, "White Heather."

"Thank you kindly, Susan," said he, as he held up the minute bottle between his big finger and thumb, and struggled with the infinitesimal cork which was too small for him to grip. "It will come in handy when I clean out the cows."

To her mother she gave a text, painted by herself, and framed in straw and woolwork.

"O Death, where is thy sting? Where, Grave, thy Victory?"

She had spent many secret hours making this, and she looked anxiously to see what her mother thought of it.

A flicker passed over Mrs. Garland's face as she kissed her cheek.

"It's very beautiful, my dear. Why did you choose the text?"

"Because it made me think of summer, of bees and wasps," replied Susan with a joyful smile.

Her father's present was a big blue handkerchief with his initials embroidered in the corner, T.G.

Then Becky brought from out of the copper tea-urn a string of blue glass beads which she had bought for Susan at Mellow and hidden for months. Mrs. Garland gave her a work-box like a house

whose roof lifted off and inside there lay little reels of black and white cotton and a tin thimble. And, most startling, the chimney was a red velvet pin-cushion!

But Joshua's present was the most wonderful. It was nothing else than the purse with mother-of-pearl sides and red lining which she had seen at Broomy Vale and coveted so long. A miracle!

Susan displayed her stocking whilst they had breakfast. She was secretly rather disappointed over the book, which was called *Three Wet Sundays*. It was obviously a Sunday book, she had only *Pilgrim's Progress* and the Bible to read on Sundays, so it was a change, but it seemed to be about some children who talked of nothing but the Israelites for three wet Sundays.

When it was wet at Windystone she played with the Noah's Ark, that blessed present of three years ago, still as good as new through being kept for Sundays only. The stags had not lost their antlers, nor the cows their horns. The spotted dogs and blue calves were just as exciting. A camel had lost his leg and walked on a matchstick, and an ostrich had broken its beak, and the ducks and swans were pale through so much swimming, but Noah and all his relations were in the best of health, and slept in their matchbox beds or sent the dove from the window or looked after the guinea-pigs which were as big as dogs.

What a book that would have made, *Three Wet Sundays in Noah's Ark*!

The postman came through the wood with a bundle of letters and Christmas cards. He stood by the fire and had a cup of tea, and admired the decorations whilst Margaret opened her letters with cries of happiness, and excitement. She didn't stop to read them,

she took out all the cards which had no names on them and popped them into envelopes. Then she readdressed them, dexterously reshuffling and redealing, so that the postman should take them with him, a thrifty procedure.

Susan had a card which she liked above everything, a church with roof and towers and foreground covered in glittering snow. But when it was held up to the light, colours streamed through the windows, reds and blues, from two patches at the back. She put it with her best treasures to be kept for ever.

It was nearly time to start for church and all was bustle and rush as usual. Margaret dressed herself in her plum-coloured merino trimmed with velvet, and dived under the bed for the bonnet-box from which she took her best bonnet and the sealskin muff. It was always wrapped up in a linen handkerchief with a sprig of lavender and lad's love, it was so precious.

Susan dragged on her brown coat running downstairs as she pulled at the sleeves, and her beaver hat with silky pompoms at the side. She wanted to kiss her father once more under the kissing-bunch before she went.

Then everybody began to run, last-minute directions about the turkey and the stuffing, hunts for threepenny-bits, for Prayer Books, for handkerchiefs and lozenges, Joshua bumping into Susan's hat, Becky letting the milk boil over, Tom shouting, "You'll be late

again, and Christmas morning," and Susan running to play "Christians Awake" in the parlour, at the last minute, but they got off before the bells began to ring.

Down the hill they went, Mrs. Garland first, Susan walking in her tracks, through the clean snow, like the page in "Good King Wenceslas," along the white roads unmarked except by the hoofs and wheels of the milk carts, to the tune of gay dancing bells to the ivy-covered church.

Inside it was warm and beautiful, with ivy and holly, and lovely lilies and red leaves from the Court. The rich people wore their silks and furs, all scented and shining. Susan looked at them and wondered about their presents. She had heard they had real Christmas trees, with toys and candles like the one in *Hans Andersen*, which stood up in a room nearly to the ceiling. She would just like to peep at one for a minute, one minute only, to see if her imagination was right.

She was almost too happy, and her heart ached with joy as she stood on a hassock by her mother's side, with her hymn-book in her hand, singing "Noel, Noel," feasting her eyes on the coloured windows and bright berries and flowers, wrapped in scents and sounds as in a cloud of incense. She buried her face in her muff in ecstasy. No thoughts of hell or idols today, only of Baby Jesus in the

manger, and the singing angels.

It was over, they went out into the sweet air, with music pouring from the organ loft, and choir-boys scrambling out of their surplices. The river ran swiftly by, with edges of ice. The yew trees spread their long branches over the white graves. Poor dead, did they know it was Christmas? Susan felt she would like to lay a present on every grave, an apple and an orange, and she looked round with interest to see the reds and yellows in the snow. She nearly ran into a gleaming silk dress, only half covered by a mantle.

Why did it stand out all by itself, like that? How did it make that lovely noise, shir-r-r, shir-r-r, like the scythe cutting down nettles?

She put out a finger and touched the ruby silk. It was colder than her own wool frock, like a dock-leaf.

Mrs. Garland had stopped to speak to someone, and Susan walked on silently in the snow, absorbed in the softness of silk and the loneliness of the dead.

It was Mrs. Drayton's dress she had touched, and she was the mother of the girls with shining hair. They had a Christmas tree, the governess had told Mrs. Garland. She must be very happy today, and Susan pressed close to her to smell the happiness.

"What a very plain child that Garland child is! Positively ugly," said Mrs. Drayton to her husband.

Susan gasped and stood still. The world was filled with sorrow. The gleaming snow was dulled, a cloud swept over the sun and the sky drooped.

Mrs. Drayton turned round and saw the girl's startled eyes.

"Will you please ask your mother to send two shillings' worth of eggs?" she said stiffly, and passed on like a queen.

"I do hope that child did not hear what you said," exclaimed Mr. Drayton nervously, for he was continually embarrassed by his wife's loud remarks.

"It will do her good," replied Mrs. Drayton calmly; "those Garlands are too independent."

Susan dropped behind; her heart ached and lay heavy in her breast. She didn't mind being called "plain," but "ugly" was like the toad, rough-skinned and venomous, which walked round the garden, or the old witch at Dangle. She was numbed by the pain.

Her mother came hurrying up and together they walked through the crisp snow by the black river, frothing over large stones in

cascades of spangles, like the lustres in Aunt Harriet's sitting-room. White boughs dipped curious fingers in the water, and gathered ice in the quiet pools. From a rock by the roadside long icicles hung, and as Susan looked at them she forgot her sorrow. There was beauty, and she climbed up to pick them, and carried them delicately in her fingers to preserve them.

She wouldn't be sad, she didn't care if she were ugly; she had accepted her wistful elfin face as she accepted the birds and trees, as something which was part of the earth.

Ice crackled under her boots as she walked along the frozen puddles and cleared away the snow with her toe. Below the surface she could see leaves and grass imprisoned like a ship in a bottle, like the soul in a man.

Mrs. Garland sent thoughts running first up the hill, little servants, to make the bread-sauce, set the table with the best dinner service, pour out elderberry wine, and baste the turkey.

Susan dragged behind, peeping at the landscape through the icicle, watching her shadow move on the snow, climb little trees and slide up walls. A friendly thing a shadow is, neither ugly nor unkind, a fantastic dancing friend.

They climbed the hill and stopped at the first gate. There was the square church tower, far away, with turrets like little black trees

growing on the corners, and above it hung all the hymns and prayers, a bunch of white clouds.

There lay the great mass of Eve's Court with little spires of soft blue smoke coming from many chimneys, like the gentle breath from a dragon's many mouths. Susan pictured the cooks and kitchen-maids, with butler and footmen, racing round, piling wood on the fires, roasting pheasants and turkeys and geese, great sirloins and haunches of venison, carrying silver dishes of jellied moulds, rainbow colour, and golden fruits, to a vast dining-room where guests sat in high-backed chairs under the shade of a Christmas tree, glittering with candles and toys.

Her own chimneys were smoking, too, blue and grey against the clear sky, and Becky was running in and out of the kitchen with the basting-spoon in one hand and the flour-dredger in the other. She would far rather be on her high hill among her own treasures than down there in the valley, with the great ones of the earth.

She suddenly remembered the message.

"Mrs. Drayton wants two shillings' worth of eggs, Mother."

"Did she mention it today? On Christmas Day? She shouldn't order eggs on Christmas Day," cried Mrs. Garland indignantly. "I always knew she was no lady."

There, Susan was vindicated. Of course Mrs. Drayton wasn't one

of the gentry. Eve's Court never called on her, everyone knew that, but she was no lady either, so she couldn't know whether Susan was ugly or not.

Susan had an infallible test for ladies. No lady turned round when she had passed. Often she had walked backwards for a mile or two, when she had been to Mellow on an errand, to see who turned round and who walked straight past with unseeing eyes.

There were very few ladies, they all turned round to look at the little girl in the grey cape, who dawdled and twisted her lonely way along the road.

There was some secret abroad, Susan felt it as soon as they got in, by the odd silence, and the knowing glances she intercepted between Joshua and her father. The house tingled with it.

"Susan, go into the parlour and bring out my concertina," said Tom, when Susan had put her gloves and Prayer Book in the bureau in the hall, and hung up her hat.

"What do you want a concertina now for, Tom?" asked Mrs.

Garland astonished, but such a flock of winks and nods flew about the room, she followed Susan across the hall.

"Mind it doesn't bite you," called Tom.

In the middle of the table was a Christmas tree, alive and growing, looking very much surprised at itself, for had not Tom dug it up from the plantation whilst they were at church, and brought it in with real snow on its branches? The rosiest of apples and the nicest yellow oranges were strung to its boughs, and some sugar biscuits with pink icing and a few humbugs from Tom's pocket lay on the snow, with a couple of gaily coloured texts and a sugar elephant. On the top of the tree shone a silver bird, a most astonishing silver glass peacock with a tail of fine feathers, which might have flown in at the window, he wouldn't say Nay and he wouldn't say Yea.

Susan was amazed. If an angel from heaven had sat on the table she would have been less surprised. She ran to hug everybody, her heart was full.

They had been so busy getting ready, for Tom only thought of it when Dan was telling him the station gossip of Mrs. Drayton's Christmas tree, they had neglected the dinner.

"Dang it," Tom had said, "we will have a Christmas tree, too. Go and get the spade, Dan."

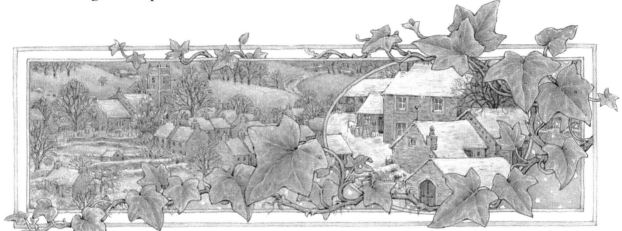

The ground had been like iron, the tree had spreading roots, but they had not harmed the little thing, and it was going back again to the plantation when Christmas was over.

The turkey was not basted, and the bread-sauce was forgotten, but everyone worked with a will and soon all was ready and piping hot.

The potatoes were balls of snow, the sprouts green as if they had just come from the garden, as indeed they had, for they too had been dug out of the snow not long before. The turkey was brown and crisp, it had been Susan's enemy for many a day, chasing her from the poultry-yard, and now it was brought low; the stuffing smelled of summer and the herb garden in the heat of the sun.

As for the plum pudding with its spray of red berries and shiny leaves and its hidden sixpence, which would fall out, and land on Susan's plate, it was the best they had ever tasted. There was no dessert, nor did they need it, for they sipped elderberry wine mixed with sugar and hot water in the old pointed wine-glasses, and cracked the walnuts damp from the trees.

Mrs. Garland, with an air of mystery, brought out *her* surprise which had lain in the parlour bedroom a few days. It was a parcel from Susan's godmother, Miss Susanna Dickory.

Tom and Susan stooped over as Mrs. Garland untied the string

and put it carefully in the string bag. It didn't do to be impatient, there was plenty of time.

There was a red shawl which Miss Dickory's old fingers had knitted for Margaret, and a grey woollen muffler and gloves to match for Tom, also knitted by Miss Dickory, and *Uncle Tom's Cabin* for Susan.

"Well, she is kind," said Margaret, "she must have worked for weeks at those things. How useful! Mind you wear those gloves, Tom. I am glad I sent her that ham. You see I was right, Tom."

"Yes," agreed Tom, "but you need not have sent a ham to Aunt Harriet, too. She never sends anything to us. It takes all our profit."

"Cast your bread upon the water," replied Margaret, and Susan looked up from the book which would soon entwine itself in her life and in her dreams. She pondered what it might mean. She never dare throw bread away, and her mother was the last person in the world to send loaves and ham floating down the river. Then she returned to the book in which she lost herself, lying before the parlour fire, until the dusk crept into the room and the firelight was insufficient even when she leaned into the fireplace.

Outside the world was amazingly blue, light blue snow, indigo trees, deep blue sky, misty blue farm and haystacks, and men with lanterns and bundles of hay on their backs for the horses and cows, or yokes across their shoulders as they went milking. Susan could hear Joshua breaking the ice on the trough by the edge of the lawn, and Duchess stood by his side waiting to drink. She lowered her great head, drank, looked around and savoured the delicious spring water on her tongue, then drank again, with snorts and soft grunts. She lifted her head and shook her mane, sending the loose

drops from her muzzle in a shower round her.

Then she whinnied contentedly and walked halterless back to the stable, lowering her head as she went under the doorway, stepping carefully up the sill. The sounds of the rope and stone weight which tethered her could be heard, as Joshua fastened her up, and then he brought out Fanny, clattering her hoofs on the floor before they were silenced in the snow.

Yellow stars like lamps, blue stars like icicles, twinkled up above and far away across the valley. A running star showed a cart or gig travelling along the coach road to Mistchester, where the cathedral stood, and the big cattle market and fine shops.

Susan pressed her nose to the cold window-pane until it became a flat white button, and her breath froze into feathery crystals. "This is Christmas Day, it's Christmas Day, it won't come again for a whole year. It's Christmas," she murmured.

The blue deepened and Becky came in to set the tea.

"Shut the shutters, Susan, and keep out the cold. You'll be fair starved by that window. They'll soon be back from milking, and I'm going to chapel tonight. I've not been for many a long bit."

Susan climbed on the leather-seated chairs and drew the folded shutters out of their niches in the depths of the walls. She racketed them across the windows, with a last long look at the deepening blue, and dropped the iron bars into the clamps.

Then she ran to the other rooms, sending out the deep clang through the shadows, which always meant cosiness and home and fireside to those within.

But outside was the wonderful Christmas night with all its mysteries, its angels busy under the stars, and seraphs singing up in Paradise.

The men rattled through the kitchen with foaming pails, for the milk did not take long to cool in the biting air which froze the drops of moisture on Joshua's whiskers, and left Tom's hands stiff and white. They stamped their feet and left great paddocks of snow on the mats by the doors and in the passage.

The mare whinnied outside the shuttered windows, as Joshua led her out, with the thick yellow and red rug across her loins. Roger barked as the churns were silently rolled through thick snow, and lifted on the cart. Joshua cried, "Coom up, lass," and led her forward, and Tom fastened the pins in the hinged back. Susan made the milk tickets, Becky polished the lamp, and Dan drank a brimming mug of tea, and hurried out into the cold night, down the deep snowy hill. He led the mare and carried a small axe in his hand with which he knocked out the great clumps of clinging snow and ice which collected in her hoofs, causing her to stumble and slip. One fall and the milk would be upset, which had happened

before now.

Becky had her tea alone in the kitchen before the fire, but old Joshua was invited to the parlour, to the feast.

There was Christmas cake, iced and sprinkled over with red and blue "hundreds and thousands," with a paper flag in the middle, on one side of which was the Union Jack and on the other a clown with a red nose and pointed hat, like the ones at the circus.

There was a fragrant ham, brother to those hanging in the kitchen corner, smoked and delicately flavoured, under its coat of brown raspings, and its paper frill which Susan had cut the night before.

There was a pie stuffed with veal, ham and eggs, potted meats in china dishes with butter on the top, brown boiled eggs in the silver egg-stand which stood like a castle with eight stalwart egg-cups and eight curling spoons round the tall handle, white bread and butter on the Minton china plates with their tiny green leaves and gold edges, a pot of honey and strawberry jam, and an old Staffordshire dish of little tarts containing golden curds made of beastings, mixed with currants.

The green and white china cups which had belonged to Mrs. Garland's grandmother were ranged at one end, beside the large teapot with its four little legs, the china sugar basin with its lid over

real crystal lumps, not brown demerara as it was Christmas, the milk jug to match, and an ancient worn silver cream jug, the "Queen Annie jug," full of thick cream which would scarcely pour out.

In the middle of the table were four silver candlesticks which were used on festal days instead of the lamp, holding four tall wax candles.

The delicate cups were passed up and down the table, the tiny plates heaped with food, Becky ran in and out with clean plates, knives and forks, with familiar jokes and smiles, as she filled up the dishes. Old Joshua ate enough for three, and then asked for more. The Christmas tree shone in the corner, and on the fire blazed a log which Becky could hardly lift when she carried it in.

The room was filled with brightness and laughter, even the shadows danced and flitted across the ceiling, four at a time, in country bobs and jigs.

They heard the sound outside of the returning cart just as the feast finished and Susan had said Grace. A piled plate with a little of everything was put ready for Dan, and Becky cleared away. Tom Garland stretched himself in the grandfather chair at one side of the fire, with his feet on the brass fender, and Joshua went out to help with the mare.

Becky washed up and cleared away before she got ready for chapel and Margaret wiped her precious china tenderly, with loving fingers and little reminiscences of when it had been used, weddings, funerals, birthdays, and Christmases.

Then Tom roused himself from his contemplation of the fire and came out to reach down the best lantern and get it ready. It hung between the old pointed horn lantern and Susan's little school lantern, a black shining case with cut-glass sides and a clean fine window at the front. He opened the back and put in a fresh piece of candle from the candle bark, and lit it.

The three set out with muffs, cloaks, walking-sticks, Prayer Books and Bibles, hymn-books, lozenges, clean handkerchiefs folded neatly, the lantern, and three pairs of old woollen stocking legs which they pulled over their boots to keep themselves from slipping. And even then Susan had to run back for the matches.

Becky walked in front with the lantern and a stick, Susan came next, and Mrs. Garland last.

There was a great conversation and warnings of snowdrifts, for the snow had fallen again in the afternoon, and the path fell away on either side so that a false step would mean a drop into the cutting down which the horse and cart had fumbled their way in deeper snow.

The lantern gave a wavering light, for Becky shook and waddled in her walk, and shadows danced about on every side. The gorse bushes which had disappeared under the drifts lay in wait for legs and ankles, and snow cluttered the uplifted skirts and petticoats.

Susan loved every moment, but Margaret and Becky were thankful when at last they reached the bottom of the long slippery hill and they had the level road in front of them.

Becky flashed her lamp over the wall, fingers of light pointing to the dark river running on its secret business, talking incessantly to itself, aloof and incomprehensible. They trudged along the turnpike, which was empty and lonely, past the milestones and the water mill, by wall and hedge, alike in the covering of snow. The church bells rang triumphantly, clear and pulsating in the stillness, racing, tumbling over one another, echoing in the hills, and then almost silent as they turned a corner and the bending river drowned the notes, or a mass of rock deflected it away. Sometimes they even caught a few notes of the bells at Brue-on-the-Water, a village far away across the hills in another valley.

In the woods above them they heard the bark of a fox. "A heathen he is," said Becky. "He should know better than to be abroad tonight," but Margaret told her foxes couldn't know, they had no souls.

The lights streamed from the church windows, straight across the graveyard, and in reds and blues the crucified Christ hung there.

"But He doesn't know about that yet," thought Susan. "He's only just born, a Baby a day old. I know more than He knows. I know He will be crucified and He doesn't know yet."

It was a disturbing thought, which shattered her as she crunched the snow under her feet and stumbled along under the church walls. She wondered if she could warn Him, tell Him to go back to Heaven, quick, before He was caught by Judas. But of course she couldn't!

It was like Charles I. She always wanted to stop him, to save him from doing the fatal things which would surely lead him, which did lead him, to the block. She was caught up in time, the present slipped behind the past. But the bells were going ting tong, ting tong, in a great hurry, as if they wanted to be quick so that they could have a Christmas mystery of their own in the sky, to count the prayers floating out of the roof and watch the cherubim catch them in their nets and carry them off to Heaven.

Becky turned away at the lych-gate, and went on to chapel where there was no jumping up and down all the time like an ill-sitting hen, but folks could lean forward with their faces in their hands and have done with it.

They blew out the lantern and took the stockings off their boots, and hid them under the stone seat in the porch.

Susan took deep sniffs, as she stood for a moment by the red baize door, of hair-oil, lavender, comfortable warm stuffs, leather leggings, paraffin and peppermint, homely smells which welcomed her in.

The lights dazzled their eyes as they walked up the aisle, Margaret gliding quietly to her place, Susan tiptoeing behind her. Lamps hung from the walls and every dark holly leaf was a candle, every scarlet berry a farthing dip. The windows alone had lost their radiance, and stood back behind the colour and warmth which filled the church, almost visible to the child's eyes searching the air for invisible things, for God on the altar, and angels floating above the choir, for music beating its wings in the high dark beams of the roof, and for goodness and mercy running hand-in-hand down the chancel.

The service was different from the morning service, too. Everybody sang mightily, the deep voices of the old men and the tiny piping voices of children overpowering the organ and compelling it to a slow grandeur in "While shepherds watched," and "Hark! the herald angels sing," and "Lead, kindly light." They wouldn't be hurried for anyone, and Samuel Robinson must slacken his pace,

going on as if he wanted to catch a train!

The old words rang out bravely, and the scent of bear's grease and peppermint balls filled the air like incense.

Susan was squeezed against her mother, close to that silky muff and the warm hand within it, by portly Mrs. Chubb who smiled and nodded and tinkled the bugles on her mantle, and shone like a crystal chandelier, besides smelling most deliciously of pear drops, which she passed to Susan when she knelt down to pray.

But the end was coming, they sang a carol, and knelt a few minutes in silence. Margaret poured out her heart to God, asking His help in the thousand anxieties which lay before her, the winter and its dangers, spring and the birds, the harvest, and Susan knelt wrapped in the beauty of the season, thinking of the Christ-Child.

Then the villagers rose to their feet and passed out of church, to greet each other in the porch and find their mufflers, sticks, and patterns. Margaret lighted the lantern and they pulled their stockings over their shoes in the confusion of the crowd. Becky waited for them at the gate, and they called, "Good night, good night. A happy Christmas and many of them. A happy Christmas and a prosperous New Year when it comes. Same to you and many of them," as they turned away to the darkness.

The snow-covered hedges, the low walls, the masses of the trees, the little paths turning to right and left, all brought a message and tried to speak to the two women and the child who walked among them, shining their lantern over them, awed by the presence of unseen things, the arch of stars above, their thoughts on God.

Susan's lips moved as she passed old friends, shrouded in white, yet intensely alive and quivering. When they reached the oak tree in the midst of the field up which they climbed, they stopped with one accord to rest.

"I was ready for my wind," said Becky, puffing.

"Stars are grand tonight," she continued. "They are candles lit by God, and however He does it I don't know."

They looked up to the light of the Milky Way, stretching across the vault of the sky, from hill to hill, from Wild Boar Head to the wood by Archer's Brow. The stars seemed alive, the air was full of

movement as they twinkled, and threw a shooting star down to the earth.

Margaret picked out the constellations, a snake with pointed head, a chair, a jewelled crown. They lost stars and found them, they put their heads together to see the same one, and pointed and cried as if they watched a show of fireworks.

But their feet were cold and they turned their eyes to the earth, and walked on up the hill towards the dark mass of buildings at the top.

"The teacher says they are other worlds," said Susan.

"We shall all know in good time," answered Margaret philosophically, "worlds or angels' eyes, or visions of heaven," and Susan decided the teacher was wrong, they were the guardian angels watching over the flocks and people who were out at night, and beyond were the golden streets and jasper walls of Heaven.

They passed under the giant beech trees, which stood very quiet with their burden of snow, by fields and hedges, to the orchard and the big gate. Roger barked and the doors flew open. They could see the square of light down the path, the radiance spread across the lawn and gilded the white laden trees.

They stamped the snow off their boots and removed the woollen coverings. Then they entered the warm fire-lit house, which

looked like Aladdin's cave with its rows of shining brass candle-sticks, its dish-covers, lustre jugs, guns, the warming-pan, and the gay decorations of holly, ivy, and flags.

The parlour table was laid for supper, Tom had been busy whilst they were away. There were mince pies, the green marbled cheese, and elderberry wine in the cut-glass decanter which had belonged to Tom's mother.

Afterwards Tom got out the concertina from its octagonal box and he dusted the tiny ivory keys and the flowered and berried sides with his silk handkerchief, gently, as if it were a child's face he was touching. Becky in great excitement gave out the hymn-books, for she dearly loved a bit of music, and she was to be invited into the room. He played his favourites of Moody and Sankey, with sweet trebles and droning basses, as they sang, in soft sad voices, tired yet happy. They knelt on the worn rose-covered carpet with their faces against the chairs, and said their prayers, putting their lives and their hopes, their seed-time and harvest, their cattle and crops in the hands of their Father.

SUNNY BANK

TRADITIONAL

As I sat on a sunny bank,
   A sunny bank, a sunny bank,
As I sat on a sunny bank
   On Christmas Day in the morning.

I saw three ships come sailing in,
   Come sailing in, come sailing in,
I saw three ships come sailing in
   On Christmas Day in the morning.

I asked them what they had in,
   What they had in, what they had in,
I asked them what they had in
   On Christmas Day in the morning.

They said they had the Saviour in,
    The Saviour in, the Saviour in,
They said they had the Saviour in,
    On Christmas Day in the morning.

I asked them where they found him,
    Where they found him, where they found him.
I asked them where they found him
    On Christmas Day in the morning.

They said they found him in Bethlehem,
    In Bethlehem, in Bethlehem,
They said they found him in Bethlehem
    On Christmas Day in the morning.

Now all the bells on earth shall ring,
    On earth shall ring, on earth shall ring,
Now all the bells on earth shall ring
    On Christmas Day in the morning.

And all the angels in heaven shall sing,
    In heaven shall sing, in heaven shall sing,
And all the angels in heaven shall sing
    On Christmas Day in the morning.

THE CHRISTMAS CUCKOO

FRANCES BROWNE

Once upon a time there stood in the midst of a bleak moor, in the north country, a certain village. All its inhabitants were poor, for their fields were barren and they had little trade; but the poorest of them all were two brothers called Scrub and Spare, who followed the cobbler's craft and had but one stall between them. It was a hut built of clay and wattles. The door was low and always open by day, for there was no window. The roof did not entirely keep out the rain and the only thing comfortable about it was a wide hearth, for which the brothers could never find wood enough to make a sufficient fire. There they worked in most brotherly friendship, though with little encouragement.

The people of that village were not extravagant in shoes, and better cobblers than Scrub and Spare might be found. Spiteful people said there were no shoes so bad that they would not be worse for their mending. Nevertheless Scrub and Spare managed

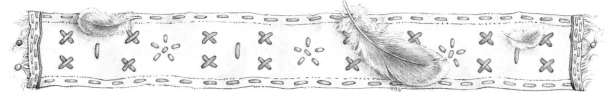

to live between their own trade, a small barley-field and a cottage garden, till one unlucky day when a new cobbler arrived in the village. He had lived in the capital city of the kingdom, and by his own account cobbled for the queen and the princesses. His awls were sharp, his lasts were new; he set up his stall in a neat cottage with two windows. The villagers soon found out that one patch of his would wear two of the brothers'. In short, all the mending left Scrub and Spare and went to the new cobbler. The season had been wet and cold, their barley did not ripen well and the cabbages never half closed in the garden. So the brothers were poor that winter, and when Christmas came they had nothing to feast on but a barley loaf, a piece of rusty bacon and some small beer of their own brewing. Worse than that, the snow was very deep and they could get no firewood. Their hut stood at the end of the village and beyond it spread the bleak moor, now all white and silent; but that moor had once been a forest and great roots of old trees were still to be found in it, loosened from the soil and laid bare by the winds and rains – one of these, a rough, gnarled log, lay hard by their door, the half of it above the snow, and Spare said to his brother:

"Shall we sit here cold on Christmas while the great root lies yonder? Let us chop it up for firewood; the work will make us warm."

"No," said Scrub; "it's not right to chop wood on Christmas; besides, that root is too hard to be broken with any hatchet."

"Hard or not we must have a fire," replied Spare. "Come, brother, help me in with it. Poor as we are, there is nobody in the village will have such a yule log as ours."

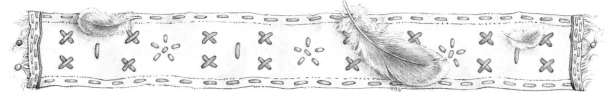

Scrub liked a little grandeur, and in hopes of having a fine yule log both brothers strained and strove with all their might till, between pulling and pushing, the great old root was safe on the hearth and beginning to crackle and blaze with the red embers. In high glee the cobblers sat down to their beer and bacon. The door was shut, for there was nothing but cold moonlight and snow outside; but the hut, strewn with fir boughs, and ornamented with holly, looked cheerful as the ruddy blaze flared up and rejoiced their hearts.

"Long life and good fortune to ourselves, brother!" said Spare. "I hope you will drink that toast, and may we never have a worse fire on Christmas – but what is that?"

Spare set down the drinking-horn, and the brothers listened astonished, for out of the blazing root they heard, "Cuckoo! cuckoo!" as plain as ever the spring-bird's voice came over the moor on a May morning.

"It is something bad," said Scrub, terribly frightened.

"Maybe not," said Spare; and out of the deep hole at the side which the fire had not reached flew a large grey cuckoo, and lit on the table before them. Much as the cobblers had been surprised, they were still more so when it said:

"Good gentlemen, what season is this?"

"It's Christmas," said Spare.

"Then a merry Christmas to you!" said the cuckoo. "I went to

sleep in the hollow of that old root one evening last summer and never woke till the heat of your fire made me think it was summer again; but now, since you have burned my lodging, let me stay in your hut till the spring comes round – I only want a hole to sleep in, and when I go on my travels next summer be assured I will bring you some present for your trouble."

"Stay, and welcome," said Spare, while Scrub sat wondering if it were something bad or not; "I'll make you a good warm hole in the thatch. But you must be hungry after that long sleep. Here is a slice of barley bread. Come, help us to keep Christmas!"

The cuckoo ate up the slice, drank water from the brown jug, for he would take no beer, and flew into a snug hole which Spare scooped for him in the thatch of the hut.

Scrub said he was afraid it wouldn't be lucky; but as it slept on and the days passed he forgot his fears. So the snow melted, the heavy rains came, the cold grew less, the days lengthened, and one sunny morning the brothers were awakened by the cuckoo shouting its own cry to let them know the spring had come.

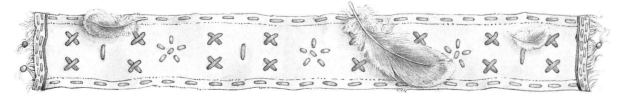

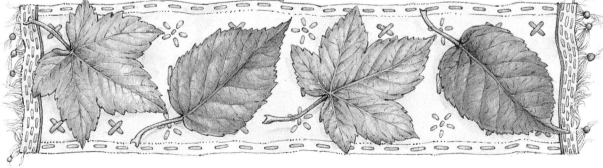

"Now I'm going on my travels," said the bird, "over the world to tell men of the spring. There is no country where trees bud or flowers bloom that I will not cry in before the year goes round. Give me another slice of barley bread to keep me on my journey and tell me what present I shall bring you at the twelvemonth's end."

Scrub would have been angry with his brother for cutting so large a slice, their store of barley-meal being low; but his mind was occupied with what present would be most prudent to ask. At length a lucky thought struck him.

"Good master cuckoo," said he, "if a great traveller who sees all the world like you, could know of any place where diamonds or pearls were to be found, one of a tolerable size brought in your beak would help such poor men as my brother and I to provide something better than barley bread for your next entertainment."

"I know nothing of diamonds or pearls," said the cuckoo; "they are in the hearts of rocks and the sands of rivers. My knowledge is only of that which grows on the earth. But there are two trees hard by the well that lies at the world's end: one of them is called the golden tree, for its leaves are all of beaten gold; every winter they fall into the well with a sound like scattered coin, and I know not what becomes of them. As for the other, it is always green like a laurel. Some call it the wise, and some the merry tree. Its leaves never fall, but they that get one of them keep a blithe heart in spite

of all misfortunes and can make themselves as merry in a hut as in a palace."

"Good master cuckoo, bring me a leaf off that tree!" cried Spare.

"Now, brother, don't be a fool!" said Scrub. "Think of the leaves of beaten gold! Dear master cuckoo, bring me one of them!"

Before another word could be spoken, the cuckoo had flown out of the open door, and was shouting its spring cry over moor and meadow. The brothers were poorer than ever that year; nobody would send them a single shoe to mend. The new cobbler said in scorn they should come to be his apprentices; and Scrub and Spare would have left the village but for their barley-field, their cabbage garden and a certain maid called Fairfeather, whom both the cobblers had courted for seven years without even knowing which she meant to favour.

Sometimes Fairfeather seemed inclined to Scrub, sometimes she smiled on Spare; but the brothers never disputed for that. They sowed their barley, planted their cabbage and, now that their trade was gone, worked in the rich villagers' fields to make out a scanty living. So the seasons came and passed: spring, summer, harvest

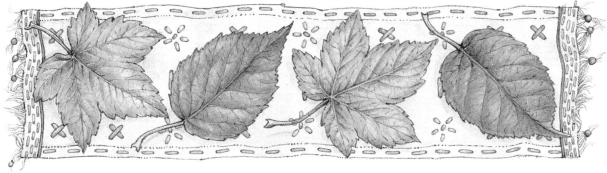

and winter followed each other as they have done from the beginning. At the end of the last, Scrub and Spare had grown so poor and ragged that Fairfeather thought them beneath her notice. Old neighbours forgot to invite them to wedding feasts or merry-making; and they thought the cuckoo had forgotten them too, when at daybreak, on the first of April, they heard a hard beak knocking at their door and a voice crying:

"Cuckoo! cuckoo! Let me in with my presents."

Spare ran to open the door, and in came the cuckoo, carrying on one side of his bill a golden leaf larger than that of any tree in the north country; and in the other, one like that of the common laurel, only it had a fresher green.

"Here," it said, giving the gold to Scrub and the green to Spare, "it is a long carriage from the world's end. Give me a slice of barley bread, for I must tell the north country that the spring has come."

Scrub did not grudge the thickness of that slice, though it was cut from their last loaf. So much gold had never been in the cobbler's hands before and he could not help exulting over his brother.

"See the wisdom of my choice!" he said, holding up the large leaf of gold. "As for yours, as good might be plucked from any hedge. I wonder a sensible bird would carry the like so far."

"Good master cobbler," cried the cuckoo, finishing the slice, "your conclusions are more hasty than courteous. If your brother be disappointed this time, I go on the same journey every year, and

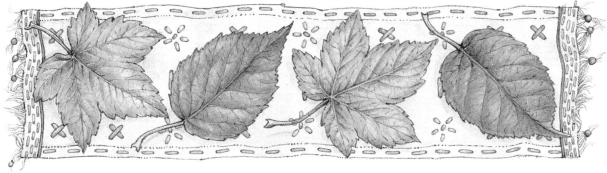

for your hospitable entertainment will think it no trouble to bring each of you whichever leaf you desire."

"Darling cuckoo," cried Scrub, "bring me a golden one"; and Spare, looking up from the green leaf on which he gazed as though it were a crown jewel, said:

"Be sure to bring me one from the merry tree," and away flew the cuckoo.

"This is the Feast of All Fools, and it ought to be your birthday," said Scrub. "Did ever man fling away such an opportunity of getting rich! Much good your merry leaves will do in the midst of rags and poverty!" So he went on, but Spare laughed at him and answered with quaint old proverbs concerning the cares that come with gold, till Scrub, at length getting angry, vowed his brother was not fit to live with a respectable man; and taking his lasts, his awls and his golden leaf, he left the wattle hut and went to tell the villagers.

They were astonished at the folly of Spare and charmed with Scrub's good sense, particularly when he showed them the golden leaf, and told that the cuckoo would bring him one every spring. The new cobbler immediately took him into partnership, the

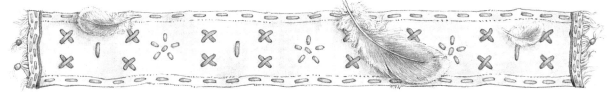

greatest people sent him their shoes to mend, Fairfeather smiled graciously upon him and in the course of that summer they were married, with a grand wedding feast, at which the whole village danced, except Spare, who was not invited, because the bride could not bear his lowmindedness, and his brother thought him a disgrace to the family.

Indeed all who heard the story concluded that Spare must be mad, and nobody would associate with him but a lame tinker, a beggar-boy and a poor woman reputed to be a witch because she was old and ugly. As for Scrub, he established himself with Fairfeather in a cottage close by that of the new cobbler, and quite as fine. There he mended shoes to everybody's satisfaction, had a scarlet coat for holidays and a fat goose for dinner every wedding-day. Fairfeather too had a crimson gown and fine blue ribands; but neither she nor Scrub were content, for to buy this grandeur the golden leaf had to be broken and parted with piece by piece, so the last morsel was gone before the cuckoo came with another.

Spare lived on in the old hut, and worked in the cabbage garden. (Scrub had got the barley-field because he was the elder.) Every day his coat grew more ragged, and the hut more weatherbeaten; but people remarked that he never looked sad nor sour; and the wonder was that, from the time they began to keep his company, the tinker grew kinder to the poor ass with which he travelled the country, the beggar-boy kept out of mischief and the old woman was never cross to her cat or angry with the children.

Every first of April the cuckoo came tapping at their doors with the golden leaf to Scrub and the green to Spare. Fairfeather would

have entertained him nobly with wheaten bread and honey, for she had some notion of persuading him to bring two gold leaves instead of one; but the cuckoo flew away to eat barley bread with Spare, saying he was not fit company for fine people, and liked the old hut where he slept so snugly from Christmas till spring.

Scrub spent the golden leaves, and Spare kept the merry ones; and I know not how many years passed in this manner, when a certain great lord who owned that village came to the neighbourhood. His castle stood on the moor. It was ancient and strong, with high towers and a deep moat. All the country, as far as one could see from the highest turret, belonged to its lord; but he had not been there for twenty years, and would not have come then, only he was melancholy. The cause of his grief was that he had been prime minister at court and in high favour, till somebody told the crown prince that he had spoken disrespectfully concerning the turning out of his royal highness's toes, and of the king that he did not lay on taxes enough, whereon the north country lord was turned out of office and banished to his own estate. There he lived for some weeks in very bad temper. The servants said nothing would please him, and the villagers put on their worst clothes lest

he should raise their rents; but one day in the harvest time his lordship chanced to meet Spare gathering watercresses at a meadow stream, and fell into talk with the cobbler.

How it was nobody could tell, but from the hour of that discourse the great lord cast away his melancholy: he forgot his lost office and his court enemies, the king's taxes and the crown prince's toes, and went about with a noble train, hunting, fishing and making merry in his hall, where all travellers were entertained and all the poor were welcome. This strange story spread through the north country, and great company came to the cobbler's hut – rich men who had lost their money, poor men who had lost their friends, beauties who had grown old, wits who had gone out of fashion – all came to talk with Spare, and whatever their troubles had been, all went home merry. The rich gave him presents, the poor gave him thanks. Spare's coat ceased to be ragged, he had bacon with his cabbage and the villagers began to think there was some sense in him.

By this time his fame had reached the capital city, and even the court. There were a great many discontented people there besides

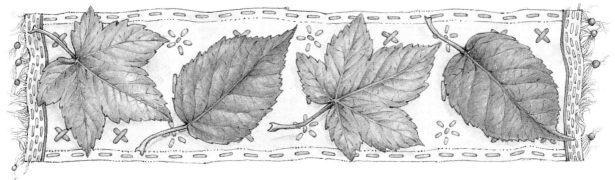

the king, who had lately fallen into ill humour because a neighbouring princess, with seven islands for her dowry, would not marry his eldest son. So a royal messenger was sent to Spare, with a velvet mantle, a diamond ring and a command that he should repair to court immediately.

"Tomorrow is the first of April," said Spare, "and I will go with you two hours after sunrise."

The messenger lodged all night at the castle, and the cuckoo came at sunrise with the merry leaf.

"Court is a fine place," he said when the cobbler told him he was going, "but I cannot come there, they would lay snares and catch me; so be careful of the leaves I have brought you, and give me a farewell slice of barley bread."

Spare was sorry to part with the cuckoo, little as he had of his company; but he gave him a slice which would have broken Scrub's heart in former times, it was so thick and large; and having sewed up the leaves in the lining of his leather doublet, he set out with the messenger on his way to court.

His coming caused great surprise there. Everybody wondered what the king could see in such a common-looking man; but scarce had his majesty conversed with him half an hour, when the princess and her seven islands were forgotten, and orders given that a feast for all comers should be spread in the banquet hall. The

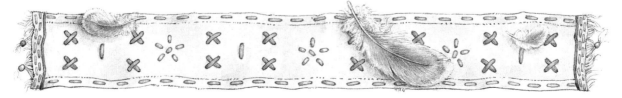

princes of the blood, the great lords and ladies, ministers of state and judges of the land, after that, discoursed with Spare, and the more they talked the lighter grew their hearts, so that such changes had never been seen at court. The lords forgot their spites and the ladies their envies, the princes and ministers made friends among themselves, and the judges showed no favour.

As for Spare, he had a chamber assigned him in the palace and a seat at the king's table; one sent him rich robes and another costly jewels; but in the midst of all his grandeur he still wore the leathern doublet, which the palace servants thought remarkably mean. One day the king's attention being drawn to it by the chief page, his majesty inquired why Spare didn't give it to a beggar? But the cobbler answered:

"High and mighty monarch, this doublet was with me before silk and velvet came – I find it easier to wear than the court cut; moreover it serves to keep me humble, by recalling the days when it was my holiday garment."

The king thought this a wise speech, and commanded that no one should find fault with the leathern doublet. So things went, till tidings of his brother's good fortune reached Scrub in the moorland cottage on another first of April, when the cuckoo came with two golden leaves, because he had none to carry for Spare.

"Think of that!" said Fairfeather. "Here we are spending our lives in this humdrum place, and Spare making his fortune at court with

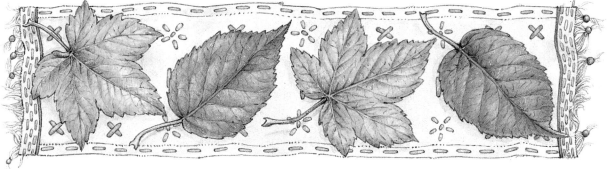

two or three paltry green leaves! What would they say to our golden ones? Let us pack up and make our way to the king's palace; I'm sure he will make you a lord and me a lady of honour, not to speak of all the fine clothes and presents we shall have."

Scrub thought this excellent reasoning, and their packing up began; but it was soon found that the cottage contained few things fit for carrying to court. Fairfeather could not think of her wooden bowls, spoons and trenchers being seen there. Scrub considered his lasts and awls better left behind, as without them, he concluded, no one would suspect him of being a cobbler. So putting on their holiday clothes, Fairfeather took her looking-glass and Scrub his drinking-horn, which happened to have a very thin rim of silver, and each carrying a golden leaf carefully wrapped up that none might see it till they reached the palace, the pair set out in great expectation.

How far Scrub and Fairfeather journeyed I cannot say, but when the sun was high and warm at noon, they came into a wood both tired and hungry.

"If I had known it was so far to court," said Scrub, "I would have brought the end of that barley loaf which we left in the cupboard."

"Husband," said Fairfeather, "you shouldn't have such mean thoughts: how could one eat barley bread on the way to a palace? Let us rest ourselves under this tree, and look at our golden leaves

to see if they are safe." In looking at the leaves, and talking of their fine prospects, Scrub and Fairfeather did not perceive that a very thin old woman had slipped from behind the tree, with a long staff in her hand and a great wallet by her side.

"Noble lord and lady," she said, "for I know you are such by your voices, though my eyes are dim and my hearing none of the sharpest, will you condescend to tell me where I may find some water to mix a bottle of mead which I carry in my wallet, because it is too strong for me?"

As the old woman spoke, she pulled out a large wooden bottle such as shepherds used in the ancient times, corked with leaves rolled together and having a small wooden cup hanging from its handle.

"Perhaps you will do me the favour to taste," she said. "It is only made of the best honey. I have also cream cheese and a wheaten loaf here, if such honourable persons as you would eat the like."

Scrub and Fairfeather became very condescending after this speech. They were now sure that there must be some appearance of nobility about them; besides, they were very hungry, and having hastily wrapped up the golden leaves, they assured the old woman they were not at all proud, notwithstanding the lands and castles they had left behind them in the north country, and would willingly help to lighten the wallet. The old woman could scarcely be

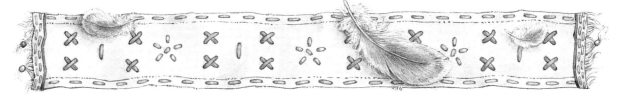

persuaded to sit down for pure humility, but at length she did, and before the wallet was half empty Scrub and Fairfeather firmly believed that there must be something remarkably noble-looking about them. This was not entirely owing to her ingenious discourse. The old woman was a wood-witch; her name was Buttertongue; and all her time was spent in making mead, which, being boiled with curious herbs and spells, had the power of making all who drank it fall asleep and dream with their eyes open. She had two dwarfs of sons; one was named Spy and the other Pounce. Wherever their mother went they were not far behind; and whoever tasted her mead was sure to be robbed by the dwarfs.

Scrub and Fairfeather sat leaning against the old tree. The cobbler had a lump of cheese in his hand; his wife held fast a hunch of bread. Their eyes and mouths were both open, but they were dreaming of great grandeur at court, when the old woman raised her shrill voice:

"What ho, my sons, come here and carry home the harvest!"

No sooner had she spoken than the two little dwarfs darted out of the neighbouring thicket.

"Idle boys!" cried the mother. "What have you done today to help our living?"

"I have been to the city," said Spy, "and could see nothing. These are hard times for us – everybody minds his business so contentedly since that cobbler came; but here is a leathern doublet which his page threw out of the window; it's of no use, but I brought it to let you see I was not idle." And he tossed down Spare's doublet, with the merry leaves in it, which he had carried like a bundle on

his little back.

To explain how Spy came by it, I must tell you that the forest was not far from the great city where Spare lived in such high esteem. All things had gone well with the cobbler till the king thought it was quite unbecoming to see such a worthy man without a servant. His majesty, therefore, to let all men understand his royal favour towards Spare, appointed one of his own pages to wait upon him. The name of this youth was Tinseltoes, and though he was the seventh of the king's pages nobody in all the court had grander notions. Nothing could please him that had not gold or silver about it, and his grandmother feared he would hang himself for being appointed page to a cobbler. As for Spare, if anything could have troubled him, this token of his majesty's kindness would have done it.

The honest man had been so used to serve himself that the page was always in the way, but his merry leaves came to his assistance; and, to the great surprise of his grandmother, Tinseltoes took wonderfully to the new service. Some said it was because Spare gave him nothing to do but play at bowls all day on the palace green. Yet one thing grieved the heart of Tinseltoes, and that was his master's leathern doublet; but for it, he was persuaded, people would never remember that Spare had been a cobbler, and the page took a deal of pains to let him see how unfashionable it was at court; but Spare answered Tinseltoes as he had done the king, and

at last, finding nothing better would do, the page got up one fine morning earlier than his master, and tossed the leathern doublet out of the back window into a certain lane where Spy found it, and brought it to his mother.

"That nasty thing!" said the old woman. "Where is the good in it?"

By this time Pounce had taken everything of value from Scrub and Fairfeather – the looking-glass, the silver-rimmed horn, the husband's scarlet coat, the wife's gay mantle, and above all the golden leaves, which so rejoiced old Buttertongue and her sons that they threw the leathern doublet over the sleeping cobbler for a jest, and went off to their hut in the heart of the forest.

The sun was going down when Scrub and Fairfeather awoke from dreaming that they had been made a lord and a lady and sat clothed in silk and velvet, feasting with the king in his palace hall. It was a great disappointment to find their golden leaves and all their best things gone. Scrub tore his hair and vowed to take the old woman's life, while Fairfeather lamented sore; but Scrub, feeling cold for want of his coat, put on the leathern doublet without asking or caring whence it came.

Scarcely was it buttoned on when a change came over him; he addressed such merry discourse to Fairfeather, that, instead of lamentations, she made the wood ring with laughter. Both busied

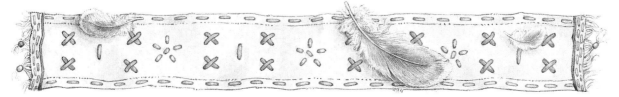

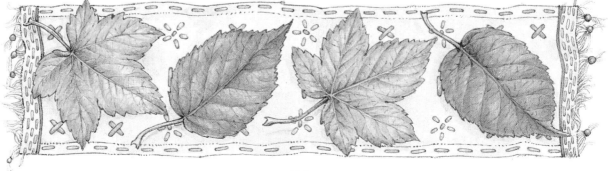

themselves in getting up a hut of boughs, in which Scrub kindled a fire with a flint and steel, which, together with his pipe, he had brought unknown to Fairfeather, who had told him the like was never heard of at court. Then they found a pheasant's nest at the root of an old oak, made a meal of roasted eggs, and went to sleep on a heap of long green grass which they had gathered, with nightingales singing all night long in the old trees about them. So it happened that Scrub and Fairfeather stayed day after day in the forest, making their hut larger and more comfortable against the winter, living on wild birds' eggs and berries and never thinking of their lost golden leaves, or their journey to court.

In the meantime Spare had got up and missed his doublet. Tinseltoes, of course, said he knew nothing about it. The whole palace was searched, and every servant questioned, till all the court wondered why such a fuss was made about an old leathern doublet. That very day things came back to their old fashion. Quarrels began among the lords and jealousies among the ladies. The king said his subjects did not pay him half enough taxes, the queen wanted more jewels, the servants took to their old bicker-ings and got up some new ones. Spare found himself getting wonderfully dull, and very much out of place: nobles began to ask what business a cobbler had at the king's table, and his majesty ordered the palace chronicles to be searched for a precedent. The cobbler was too wise to tell all he had lost with that doublet, but

being by this time somewhat familiar with court customs, he proclaimed a reward of fifty gold pieces to any who would bring him news concerning it.

Scarcely was this made known in the city when the gates and outer courts of the palace were filled by men, women and children, some bringing leathern doublets of every cut and colour – some with tales of what they had heard and seen in their walks about the neighbourhood. And so much news concerning all sorts of great people came out of these stories that lords and ladies ran to the king with complaints of Spare as a speaker of slander; and his majesty, being now satisfied that there was no example in all the palace records of such a retainer, issued a decree banishing the cobbler for ever from court and confiscating all his goods in favour of Tinseltoes.

That royal edict was scarcely published before the page was in full possession of his rich chamber, his costly garments and all the presents the courtiers had given him; while Spare, having no longer the fifty pieces of gold to give, was glad to make his escape out of the back window, for fear of the nobles, who vowed to be

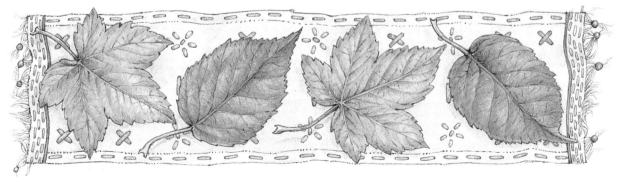

revenged on him, and the crowd, who were prepared to stone him for cheating them about his doublet.

The window from which Spare let himself down with a strong rope was that from which Tinseltoes had tossed the doublet, and as the cobbler came down late in the twilight, a poor woodman with a heavy load of faggots stopped and stared at him in great astonishment.

"What's the matter, friend?" said Spare. "Did you never see a man coming down from a back window before?"

"Why," said the woodman, "the last morning I passed here a leathern doublet came out of that very window, and I'll be bound you are the owner of it."

"That I am, friend," said the cobbler. "Can you tell me which way that doublet went?"

"As I walked on," said the woodman, "a dwarf, called Spy, bundled it up and ran off to his mother in the forest."

"Honest friend," said Spare, taking off the last of his fine clothes (a grass-green mantle edged with gold), "I'll give you this if you will follow the dwarf and bring me back my doublet."

"It would not be good to carry faggots in," said the woodman. "But if you want back your doublet, the road to the forest lies at the end of this lane," and he trudged away.

Determined to find his doublet, and sure that neither crowd nor courtiers could catch him in the forest, Spare went on his way, and

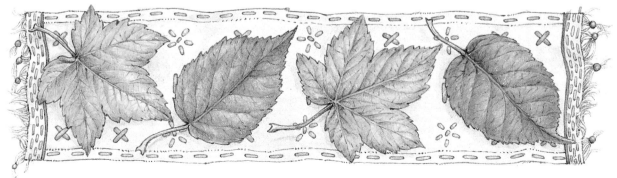

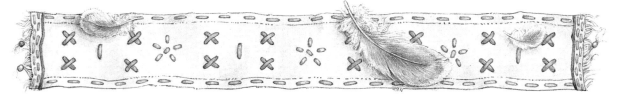

was soon among the tall trees; but neither hut nor dwarf could he see. Moreover the night came on; the wood was dark and tangled, but here and there the moon shone through its alleys, the great owls flitted about, and the nightingales sang. So he went on, hoping to find some place of shelter. At last the red light of a fire, gleaming through a thicket, led him to the door of a low hut. It stood half open, as if there was nothing to fear, and within he saw his brother Scrub snoring loudly on a bed of grass, at the foot of which lay his own leathern doublet; while Fairfeather, in a kirtle made of plaited rushes, sat roasting pheasants' eggs by the fire.

"Good evening, mistress," said Spare, stepping in.

The blaze shone on him, but so changed was her brother-in-law with his court life, that Fairfeather did not know him, and she answered far more courteously than was her wont.

"Good evening, master. Whence come ye so late? But speak low, for my good man has sorely tired himself cleaving wood, and is taking a sleep, as you see, before supper."

"A good rest to him," said Spare, perceiving he was not known. "I come from the court for a day's hunting, and have lost my way in the forest."

"Sit down and have a share of our supper," said Fairfeather. "I will put some more eggs in the ashes; and tell me the news of court – I used to think of it long ago when I was young and foolish."

"Did you never go there?" said the cobbler. "So fair a dame as

you would make the ladies marvel."

"You are pleased to flatter," said Fairfeather; "but my husband has a brother there, and we left our moorland village to try our fortune also. An old woman enticed us with fair words and strong drink at the entrance of this forest, where we fell asleep and dreamt of great things; but when we woke, everything had been robbed from us – my looking-glass, my scarlet cloak, my husband's Sunday coat; and, in place of all, the robbers left him that old leathern doublet, which he has worn ever since, and never was so merry in all his life, though we live in this poor hut."

"It is a shabby doublet, that," said Spare, taking up the garment, and seeing that it was his own, for the merry leaves were still sewed in its lining. "It would be good for hunting in, however – your husband would be glad to part with it, I dare say, in exchange for this handsome cloak"; and he pulled off the green mantle and buttoned on the doublet, much to Fairfeather's delight, who ran and shook Scrub, crying:

"Husband! husband! rise and see what a good bargain I have made!"

Scrub gave one closing snore, and muttered something about the root being hard; but he rubbed his eyes, gazed up at his brother, and said:

"Spare, is that really you? How did you like the court, and have you made your fortune?"

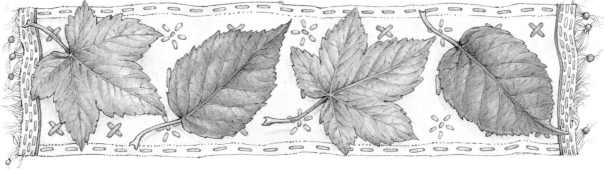

"That I have, brother," said Spare, "in getting back my own good leathern doublet. Come, let us eat eggs and rest ourselves here this night. In the morning we will return to our own old hut, at the end of the moorland village where the Christmas Cuckoo will come and bring us leaves."

Scrub and Fairfeather agreed. So in the morning they all returned, and found the old hut the worse for wear and weather. The neighbours came about them to ask the news of court, and see if they had made their fortune. Everybody was astonished to find the three poorer than ever, but somehow they liked to go back to the hut. Spare brought out the lasts and awls he had hidden in a corner; Scrub and he began their old trade, and the whole north country found out that there never were such cobblers.

They mended the shoes of lords and ladies as well as the common people; everybody was satisfied. Their custom increased from day to day, and all that were disappointed, discontented or unlucky came to the hut as in old times before Spare went to court.

The rich brought them presents, the poor did them service. The hut itself changed, no one knew how. Flowering honeysuckle grew over its roof; red and white roses grew thick about its door. Moreover the Christmas Cuckoo always came on the first of April, bringing three leaves of the merry tree – for Scrub and Fairfeather would have no more golden ones. So it was with them when I last heard the news of the north country.

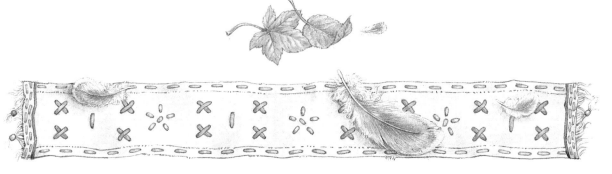

THE HOLLY AND THE IVY

TRADITIONAL

The holly and the ivy,
When they are both full grown,
Of all the trees that are in the wood,
The holly bears the crown.

O the rising of the sun,
And the running of the deer,
The playing of the merry organ,
Sweet singing in the choir.

The holly bears a blossom,
As white as the lily flower,
And Mary bore sweet Jesus Christ,
To be our sweet Saviour.

The holly bears a berry,
As red as any blood,
And Mary bore sweet Jesus Christ,
To do poor sinners good.

The holly bears a prickle,
As sharp as any thorn,
And Mary bore sweet Jesus Christ,
On Christmas Day in the morn.

The holly bears a bark,
As bitter as any gall,
And Mary bore sweet Jesus Christ,
For to redeem us all.

O the rising of the sun,
And the running of the deer,
The playing of the merry organ,
Sweet singing in the choir.

FROM THE GOSPEL
OF ST. LUKE

CHAPTER 2, VERSES 1-20

And it came to pass in those days, that there went out a decree from Caesar Augustus, that all the world should be taxed.

(And this taxing was first made when Cyrenius was governor of Syria.)

And all went to be taxed, every one into his own city.

And Joseph also went up from Galilee, out of the city of Nazareth, into Judaea, unto the city of David, which is called Bethlehem; (because he was of the house and lineage of David:)

To be taxed with Mary his espoused wife, being great with child.

And so it was, that, while they were there, the days were accomplished that she should be delivered.

And she brought forth her first-born son, and wrapped him in swaddling clothes, and laid him in a manger; because there was no room for them in the inn.

And there were in the same country shepherds abiding in the field, keeping watch over their flock by night.

And, lo, the angel of the Lord came upon them, and the glory of the Lord shone round about them: and they were sore afraid.

And the angel said unto them, Fear not: for, behold, I bring you good tidings of great joy, which shall be to all people.

For unto you is born this day in the city of David a Saviour, which is Christ the Lord.

And this shall be a sign unto you; Ye shall find the babe wrapped in swaddling clothes, lying in a manger.

And suddenly there was with the angel a multitude of the heavenly host praising God, and saying,

Glory to God in the highest, and on earth peace, good will toward men.

And it came to pass, as the angels were gone away from them into heaven, the shepherds said one to another, Let us now go even unto Bethlehem, and see this thing which is come to pass, which the Lord hath made known unto us.

And they came with haste, and found Mary, and Joseph, and the babe lying in a manger.

And when they had seen it, they made known abroad the saying which was told them concerning this child.

And all they that heard it wondered at those things which were told them by the shepherds.

But Mary kept all these things, and pondered them in her heart.

And the shepherds returned, glorifying and praising God for all the things that they had heard and seen, as it was told unto them.

CAROL OF THE BROWN KING

LANGSTON HUGHES

Of the three Wise Men
Who came to the King,
One was a brown man,
So they sing.

Of the three Wise Men
Who followed the Star,
One was a brown king
From afar.

They brought fine gifts
Of spices and gold
In jewelled boxes
Of beauty untold.

Unto His humble
Manger they came
And bowed their heads
In Jesus' name.

Three Wise Men,
One dark like me –
Part of His
Nativity.

LULLAY, MY LIKING

ANONYMOUS

Adapted from a fifteenth-century carol

Lullay, my liking, my son, my sweeting.
Lullay, my dear heart, my own dear darling.

I saw a fair maiden
Sit and sing:
She lulled a little child,
A sweet lording.

He is that Lord
Who made every thing:
Of all lords the Lord,
Of all kings the King.

There was much song
At that child's birth:
All those in heaven,
They made much mirth.

Angels bright, they sung that night,
And said to that child:
"Blessed be thou and so be she,
That is both meek and mild."

Pray we now to that child
And to his mother dear,
To bless us all
Who now make cheer.

Lullay, my liking, my son, my sweeting.
Lullay, my dear heart, my own dear darling.

HARK! THE HERALD ANGELS SING

CHARLES WESLEY

Hark! the herald angels sing,
Glory to the new-born King.
Peace on earth, and mercy mild,
God and sinners reconciled.
Joyful, all you nations rise,
Join the triumph of the skies.
With the angelic hosts proclaim,
"Christ is born in Bethlehem."

Hark! the herald angels sing,
"Glory to the new-born King."

Christ, by highest heaven adored,
Christ, the everlasting Lord,
Late in time behold him come,
Offspring of a Virgin's womb.
Veiled in flesh the Godhead see;
Hail, the Incarnate Deity,
Pleased as Man with man to dwell,
Jesus, our Emmanuel!

Hark! the herald angels sing,
"Glory to the new-born King."

Hail, the heaven-born Prince of Peace!
Hail, the Sun of Righteousness!
Light and life to all he brings,
Risen with healing in his wings.
Mild he lays his glory by,
Born that man no more may die,
Born to raise the sons of earth,
Born to give them second birth.

Hark! the herald angels sing,
"Glory to the new-born King."

141

THE CAT ON THE DOVREFELL

A NORWEGIAN FOLKTALE

Translated by Sir George Webbe Dasent

Once on a time there was a man up in Finnmark who had caught a great white bear, which he was going to take to the king of Denmark. Now, it so fell out, that he came to the Dovrefell just about Christmas Eve, and there he turned into a cottage where a man lived, whose name was Halvor, and asked the man if he could get house-room there, for his bear and himself.

"Heaven never help me, if what I say isn't true!" said the man; "but we can't give any one house-room just now, for every Christmas Eve such a pack of Trolls come down upon us, that we are forced to flit, and haven't so much as a house over our own heads, to say nothing of lending one to anyone else."

"Oh?" said the man, "if that's all, you can very well lend me your house; my bear can lie under the stove yonder, and I can sleep in the side-room."

Well, he begged so hard, that at last he got leave to stay there; so the people of the house flitted out, and before they went, everything was got ready for the Trolls; the tables were laid, and there was rice porridge, and fish boiled in lye, and sausages, and all else that was good, just as for any other grand feast.

So, when everything was ready, down came the Trolls. Some were great and some were small; some had long tails, and some had no tails at all; some, too, had long, long noses; and they ate and drank, and tasted everything. Just then, one of the little Trolls caught sight of the white bear, who lay under the stove; so he took a piece of sausage and stuck it on a fork, and went and poked it up against the bear's nose, screaming out —

"Pussy, will you have some sausage?"

Then the white bear rose up and growled, and hunted the whole pack of them out of doors, both great and small.

Next year Halvor was out in the wood, on the afternoon of Christmas Eve, cutting wood before the holidays, for he thought

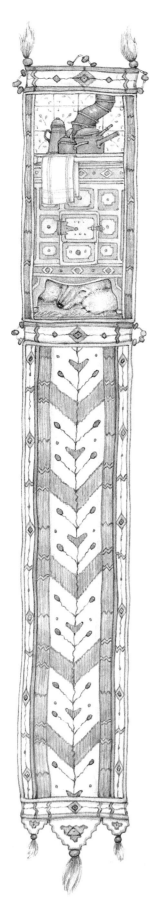

the Trolls would come again; and just as he was hard at work, he heard a voice in the wood calling out, —

"Halvor! Halvor!"

"Well," said Halvor, "here I am."

"Have you got your big cat with you still?"

"Yes, that I have," said Halvor; "she's lying at home under the stove, and what's more, she has now got seven kittens, far bigger and fiercer than she is herself."

"Oh, then, we'll never come to see you again," bawled out the Troll away in the wood, and he kept his word; for since that time the Trolls have never eaten their Christmas brose with Halvor on the Dovrefell.

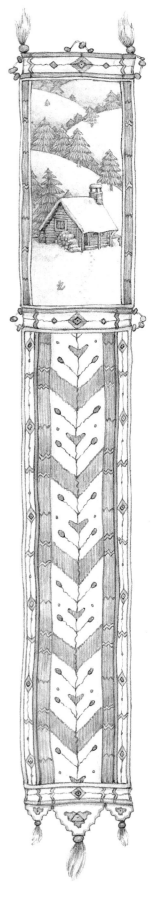

THE TWELVE DAYS
OF CHRISTMAS

TRADITIONAL

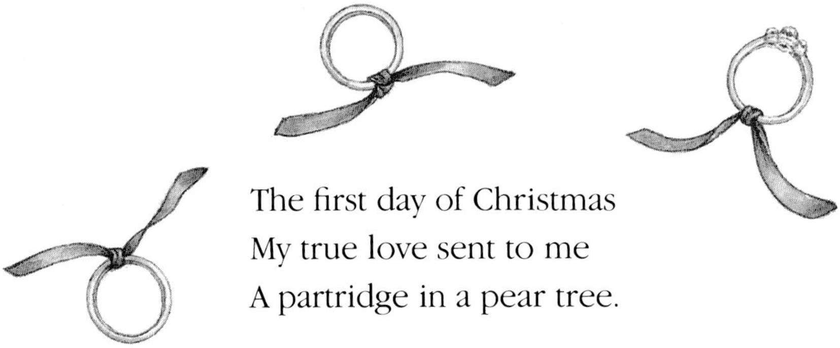

The first day of Christmas
My true love sent to me
A partridge in a pear tree.

The second day of Christmas
My true love sent to me
Two turtle doves, and
A partridge in a pear tree.

The third day of Christmas
My true love sent to me
Three French hens,
Two turtle doves, and
A partridge in a pear tree.

The fourth day of Christmas
My true love sent to me
Four colly birds,
Three French hens,
Two turtle doves, and
A partridge in a pear tree.

The fifth day of Christmas
My true love sent to me
Five gold rings,
Four colly birds,
Three French hens,
Two turtle doves, and
A partridge in a pear tree.

The sixth day of Christmas
My true love sent to me
Six geese a-laying,
Five gold rings,
Four colly birds,
Three French hens,
Two turtle doves, and
A partridge in a pear tree.

The seventh day of Christmas
My true love sent to me
Seven swans a-swimming,
Six geese a-laying,
Five gold rings,

Four colly birds,
Three French hens,
Two turtle doves, and
A partridge in a pear tree.

The eighth day of Christmas
My true love sent to me
Eight maids a-milking,
Seven swans a-swimming,
Six geese a-laying,
Five gold rings,
Four colly birds,
Three French hens,
Two turtle doves, and
A partridge in a pear tree.

The ninth day of Christmas
My true love sent to me
Nine drummers drumming,
Eight maids a-milking,
Seven swans a-swimming,
Six geese a-laying,
Five gold rings,
Four colly birds,
Three French hens,
Two turtle doves, and
A partridge in a pear tree.

The tenth day of Christmas
My true love sent to me
Ten pipers piping,
Nine drummers drumming,
Eight maids a-milking,
Seven swans a-swimming,
Six geese a-laying,
Five gold rings,
Four colly birds,
Three French hens,
Two turtle doves, and
A partridge in a pear tree.

The eleventh day of Christmas
My true love sent to me
Eleven ladies dancing,
Ten pipers piping,
Nine drummers drumming,
Eight maids a-milking,
Seven swans a-swimming,
Six geese a-laying,
Five gold rings,
Four colly birds,
Three French hens,
Two turtle doves, and
A partridge in a pear tree.

The twelfth day of Christmas
My true love sent to me

Twelve lords a-leaping,
Eleven ladies dancing,
Ten pipers piping,
Nine drummers drumming,

Eight maids a-milking,
Seven swans a-swimming,
Six geese a-laying,
Five gold rings,

Four colly birds,
Three French hens,
Two turtle doves, and

A partridge in a pear tree.

THE LITTLE MATCH GIRL

HANS CHRISTIAN ANDERSEN

English version by Neil Philip

It was bitter cold and snowing hard, and it was almost dark; the last evening of the old year was drawing in. But despite the cold and dark, one poor little girl was still astray in the streets, with nothing on her head and nothing on her feet. She had had slippers on when she left home, but they were her mother's and were too big for her, and they had dropped from her feet when she scampered across the road between two carriages. One slipper just disappeared, and the other was snatched away by a little boy, who wanted it as a doll's cradle.

So the little girl walked on, and her bare feet turned blue and raw with the cold. In her hand she carried a bundle of matches, and there were more in her ragged apron. No one had bought any matches the livelong day; no one had given her so much as a penny. And so she walked on, shivering and starved, poor girl.

The snowflakes fell on her long blond hair, which curled so prettily on her shoulders. But she was not thinking of her beauty, nor of the cold, for lights were winking from every window, and

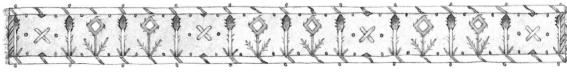

the savour of roast goose was in the air. It was New Year's Eve, and that was what the girl was thinking of.

She sat down in a sheltered corner and snuggled her feet under her, but it was no use. She couldn't get them warm. She didn't dare go home, for she had sold no matches, and not earned so much as a penny. Her father would probably beat her, and anyway her home was nearly as cold as the street. It was an attic, and despite the straw and rags which filled the worst of the holes in the roof, the wind and snow still whistled through it. Her hands were numb with cold. If only she dared strike a single match, perhaps that would warm them. She took one out, and struck it on the wall. Ah! The flame was bright and warm, and she held her hands to it. It burned for her with a magic light, till it seemed as if she were sitting by a great iron stove, with a lovely fire burning in it. The girl stretched out her feet to warm them too, but oh! The flame died down. The stove was gone, and the little girl was frozen and alone, with the burnt match in her hand.

She struck a second match against the wall. It flamed, and wherever its light fell the wall thinned to a veil so that the little girl could see into the room within. She saw a table spread with a snow-white cloth all set with fine china, and a piping hot roast goose stuffed with apples and plums. Best of all, the goose, with the knife and fork still in its breast, jumped down from the dish, and waddled along the floor right up to the poor child. Then the match burnt out, and the girl was left beside the cold, thick wall.

She kindled another match. Now she was sitting under a lovely Christmas tree, far bigger and more beautifully decorated than the one she had peeped at through the glass doors of a rich merchant's house last Christmas. A thousand candles were glimmering in the branches, and little painted figures, such as she had seen in shop windows, were looking down at her from the tree. The girl reached out her hands towards them, and the match went out. But still the Christmas candles burned higher and higher; she could see them twinkling like stars in the sky. Then one of them fell, leaving a trail of fiery light.

"Now someone is dying," said the little girl, for her grandmother, who was the only person who had been kind to her, but who was now dead, had told her that when a star falls, a soul is going to God.

She struck another match against the wall. It lit, and there, clear and bright in its glow, stood her old grandmother, as gentle and loving as ever.

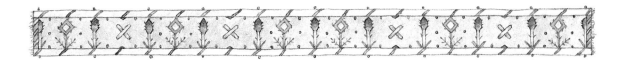

"Grandmother," shouted the little girl. "Take me with you! I know you will leave me when the match goes out. You will vanish like the warm stove, the delicious roast goose and the beautiful big Christmas tree!" Feverishly the girl struck all the rest of the matches in her bundle, to keep her grandmother there. The matches blazed with the radiance of bright sunshine. Never had Grandmother looked so beautiful and so tall. She lifted the little girl in her arms, and they flew together in glory and joy, higher and higher, beyond cold, beyond hunger, beyond fear, to God.

They found her in the early morning, sitting in the corner of the wall with rosy cheeks and a smile on her lips, frozen to death on the last night of the old year. The new year's sun rose over the little body, sitting with one bundle of her matches all burned out. "She was trying to warm herself," people said; but no one knew what beautiful visions she had seen, nor how gloriously she and her grandmother were seeing in the glad new year.

SILENT NIGHT

JOSEPH MOHR

Silent night, holy night,
All is calm, all is bright,
Round yon' Virgin mother and child,
Holy infant so tender and mild,
Sleep in heavenly peace,
Sleep in heavenly peace.

Silent night, holy night,
Shepherds quake at the sight;
Glory streams from heaven afar,
Heavenly hosts sing Alleluia.
Christ the Saviour is born!
Christ the Saviour is born!

Silent night, holy night,
Son of God, love's pure light;
Radiance beams from thy holy face,
With the dawn of redeeming grace,
Jesus, Lord at thy birth,
Jesus, Lord at thy birth.

ACKNOWLEDGMENTS

*We are indebted to the copyright holders
for permission to reproduce the following:*

Hans Christian Andersen: "The Snowman" translated by Brian Alderson, from THE PINK FAIRY BOOK by Andrew Lang, translation copyright © Brian Alderson 1982, reproduced by permission of Penguin Books Ltd. "The Little Match Girl" English version by Neil Philip copyright © Neil Philip 1991.

e.e. cummings: "little tree" from COMPLETE POEMS 1936-1962, reproduced by permission of Grafton Books, part of HarperCollins Publishers, and "little tree" from TULIPS & CHIMNEYS, edited by George James Firmage, reproduced by permission of Liveright Publishing Corporation. Copyright 1923, 1925 and renewed 1951, 1953 by e.e. cummings. Copyright © 1973, 1976 by the Trustees for the e.e. cummings Trust. Copyright © 1973, 1976 by George James Firmage.

Elizabeth Enright: "A Christmas Tree for Lydia" reproduced by permission of A.M. Heath & Company Ltd.

Langston Hughes: "Carol of the Brown King" from SELECTED POEMS OF LANGSTON HUGHES © 1958 by Crisis Publishing Co, © renewed 1986 by George Houston Bass.

Traditional: "Winter's Song" from THE BOOK OF A THOUSAND POEMS published by Evans Brothers Ltd, 1959.

Alison Uttley: "Christmas Day" from THE COUNTRY CHILD reproduced by permission of Faber and Faber Ltd.

*Every effort has been made to trace copyright holders. The Albion Press, in care of the publishers, would be
interested to hear from any copyright holders not here acknowledged.*